A CHRISTMAS TO REMEMBER

Listen to the memories…you can almost hear the sound of bells tinkling on the horse-drawn sleigh as it crackles across a snow-crusted path…sniff the perfume of pine and spruce in the frosty air…and see your friends and neighbors waving with warm wishes as you pass by.

Christmas is a time for remembering, and this book contains all the makings for a most memorable holiday. You'll find recipes for delicious dinners and desserts…a flurry of crafts (from stenciled greeting cards to a crocheted stocking)…traditional Christmas carols…and touching true stories of hope and inspiration by folks who discovered firsthand that the best Christmas gifts are those that come from the heart.

Like the wonder of that very first Christmas—the real reason for the season—nearly 2,000 years ago, holiday memories don't fade with time. They become more precious. So enjoy the memories…and may this Christmas be one you'll remember always!

Editor
Linda Piepenbrink

Art Director
Doris Schaffer

Art Associate
Cindy Weber

Food Editor
Mary Beth Jung

Test Kitchen Assistant
Denise Simeth

Craft Editors
Tricia Coogan, Kathy Rankin

Assistant Editor
Kristine Krueger

Production
Ellen Lloyd
Julie Wagner

**Cover, Craft and
 Food Photography**
Mike Huibregtse

Director of Food Photography
Bonnie Ziolecki

©1992, Reiman Publications, L.P.
5400 S. 60th Street
Greendale WI 53129

International Standard
 Book Number: 0-89821-100-X
Library of Congress Catalog
 Card Number: 92-60714

CONTENTS

Pictured on our cover: Father Christmas
(p. 82), Cross-Stitched Peppermint Jar (p. 39),
Good King Wenceslas (p. 49), Gingerbread
Cookies (p. 29), Almond Butter Crunch Candy
(p. 33), Emma's Christmas Braid (p. 22).

TREASURED TRADITIONS

Make the season bright...consider adopting a few of these inspirations for your own family.

FOOD FOR THOUGHT

YEARS AGO, I wanted our children to appreciate the real reason we celebrate on December 25. So I decided to bake a birthday cake for Jesus.

That became a family tradition that's lasted over 30 years! Now, when our children and grandchildren visit for the holidays, we always have a birthday cake. On Christmas Eve, we light the candles and sing "Happy Birthday" to Jesus.

Surprisingly, when I mention birthday cake at Christmastime, friends often ask, "Whose birthday is it?" But our children and grandchildren have no doubt about what event we're celebrating!

Margaret Carr, Arcola, Saskatchewan

ADVENT BRINGS TOGETHERNESS

WE MAKE our holiday season special by planning a family activity for every day during December. On a Christmas-tree-shaped calendar cut from green poster board, I mark off 25 daily sections, and in each section we write down something to do that day.

Beginning December 1, we make cookies or candy...one day we invite an elderly neighbor for a meal...the next we visit a nursing home with little gifts for each resident...we sing Christmas carols one evening...drive around to look at lights the next, etc.

Also during the month, each of us works on a handmade gift for someone special. And together we make spice balls and popcorn garlands.

By taking time out, we're building happy memories for our children.

Karen Ellis
Clermont, Iowa

HOLIDAY OPENS THEIR HEARTS

BEFORE opening gifts on Christmas morning, we always pause to "open our hearts". First Daddy reads the Christmas story from the Bible...then another member of the family says a special prayer... and we conclude by singing "Happy Birthday" to Jesus.

Once we have our hearts opened to the true meaning of Christmas, the gifts are passed out in honor of our Lord's birthday. This tradition reminds us that Christmas is not just a holiday, but a *holy* day as well.

Joyce A. Cutting, Hardy, Virginia

OLD ORNAMENTS, NEW MEMORIES

OUR most-loved family Christmas tradition started when our three children were small.

Every year, I bought each of them a new tree ornament, and kept a list of the year it was purchased.

Then, the first Christmas after each child married, I gave them all their ornaments along with the list. That gave them a nice start on their own Christmas decorations...plus lots of memories to carry to their new homes.

Betty Combs, De Smet
South Dakota

MATCHING GIFTS

WE'VE carried on a tradition that my parents started. We keep track of just how much we spend on each other at Christmas—and then we donate the same amount to needy area families!

Ginny Sauder, Denver, Pennsylvania

PHOTOS ARE FUN

MY PARENTS have had Christmas cards made from a family photo every year for 40 years. Getting together for a new photo each year is a family tradition.

Looking through all the old cards together is a tradition, too. It's so much fun to see how fashions, hairdos—and all of us children plus our spouses and children—have changed over the years!

Kaye Dinsmore, Belvidere, Illinois

SANTA ALWAYS LEAVES HIS MARK

THE GRANDCHILDREN always know Santa's arrived at our house. The first things they look for when they visit on Christmas are his snowy footprints!

Just before those youngsters arrive, I put a little flour in a pan... dip a shoe in it...and pat white footprints on the rug.

Later, when no one's looking, I rub in the flour to make it look like the snow's melted. Then I vacuum it up the next day!

Jodie McCoy, Tulsa, Oklahoma

Do You Remember
CHRISTMAS PAST?

BY LINDA PIEPENBRINK
MILWAUKEE, WISCONSIN

What was Christmas like when you were young?" I asked my parents recently. Their eyes lit up with the memories still fresh in their minds after so many years. But it wasn't the presents or festive feasts that my parents reminisced about. Their most vivid recollections center around going to church to celebrate the new-born King's birth.

Before my father's papa could afford a Model T, for example, his family crowded into a horse-drawn surrey for the 3-mile ride to a small church in rural Missouri for Christmas Eve services. As the stars twinkled above, they sang their favorite hymns by memory: *Oh Little Town of Bethlehem*, *The First Noel* and others.

They Got to the Church on Time!

Christmas or not, going to church was a matter of faithfulness—even on cold days when the Model T they finally acquired wouldn't start. "It didn't matter if it was 10 degrees outside," Dad recalls. "My father would simply hitch a couple of horses to the car and drag it around in gear until the car warmed up enough to start!"

Besides receiving a bag of candy and an orange (the only orange Dad got all year!) at church, the biggest highlight for my father came after the sermon. That's when a few of the elders lit the 50 or so candles on the fragrant 14-foot cedar tree, which was all dressed up in colored rope, tinsel and home-made ornaments. The men stood nearby with sticks tied with water-soaked rags to keep the tree (cedar burns easily!) from catching fire.

"When the candles burned down, the men had to put them out lickety-split before they ignited the tree," my father explains. "As a boy, I always hoped they wouldn't be able to put one out in time…but they always did," he adds with a mischievous grin.

Mom Loved Services, Too

My mother, the daughter of a minister, also looks back fondly at the people-packed Christmas Eve services in her Wisconsin hometown. That's when both of her parents sat in the audience as she and her classmates performed songs and a Nativity program they'd practiced for weeks.

"One year we sang *Angels We Have Heard on High*, and I thought that was the most heavenly piece I'd ever heard," she says.

As an only child, my mother enjoyed all the excitement with her friends and hated to see the evening end.

"As I got a little older," my mother recalls, "I wrote to Santa Claus every year and said, 'Please don't bring me any gifts this year…just a baby brother or sister.'"

My dear mother didn't get *that* wish granted, but eventually she and my father were blessed with seven children and many more grandchildren. And together, our large family has continued to share many joyful Christmases to remember.

GOOD THINGS COME IN SMALL PACKAGES

CHRISTMAS IS a time for joys,
a time for happy girls and boys,
dressed in red and Santa smiles,
like a postcard 'cross the miles.
When kids celebrate the season,
there is nothing quite as pleasin'!

HO-HO-HO! *Jacob Gogean brightened hearts with this pose,* Grandma Martha Magoto of Russia, Ohio writes. *"It's plain to see he was enjoying his first Christmas."*

DOG DAYS OF DECEMBER. *The irresistible gift of a puppy would gladden any child's Christmas morning, especially when it's as appealing as this little golden Lab!*

CHRISTMAS THREE. *"Our twin daughters and daughter-in-law each presented us with a granddaughter during the summer of 1987,"* writes Mrs. Ken Henschel of Kiel, Wisconsin. *"Needless to say, it was a very merry Christmas at our place that year!"*

"BETTER NOT POUT!" *Briston Pritchard reminds her twin, Philip. She in her kerchief, he in his cap were caught by* Grandma Wanda Sheppard of Benton, Kentucky.

WHAT A CARD. *"Our cow 'Valerie' is a very gentle Jersey,"* says Cindy Kentner of Jasper, Missouri. *"So Darrell, I and our children—Kelly, Matthew and Jaimee—dressed up and posed like this for our Christmas card."* Valerie never moo-ved!

Santa Claus Is Coming...
TO THE COUNTRY!

BY JANIE PINKHAM, BRISTOL, WEST VIRGINIA

Two years ago, a few weeks before Christmas, our 3-year-old son, Johnathan, came to me and asked if we lived in the country or in town. I assured him that we lived in the country.

He immediately asked if we could move to town, saying he didn't want to live in the country anymore! Rather surprised by his request, I reminded him that if we moved to town he wouldn't be able to keep his pet goat, "Andy", the baby calves, our barnful of cats, his pig or his pony or any of the other animals he loved.

When Johnathan considered that, he agreed that he didn't want to move, and went off to play with his 5-year-old sister, Amy Jo. For the next few days, I never gave the conversation another thought.

The following week was filled with Christmas preparation. The kids practiced their parts for the Sunday school program and never missed a chance to sit on Santa's lap when we went Christmas shopping. They busily helped me wrap packages and do the decorating, and sang heartily whenever *Away in the Manger* and *Jingle Bells* came on the radio. Johnathan was learning to sing, and the words stuck perfectly in his mind.

"He told me that he didn't want to live in the country anymore."

A few days before Christmas, though, I overheard Johnathan ask his dad if we lived in the country. My husband, George, very proudly assured him that we did. Johnathan again expressed his interest in moving to town.

George used the same approach I had used, naming all the animals we would have to leave behind if we moved.

A few minutes later I sensed my little guy standing behind me as I was fixing dinner. When I looked down, I saw tears in his big brown eyes and spilling down onto his cheeks. Johnathan's lower lip was pushed out and trembling.

When I asked him what was wrong, he repeated that he didn't want to live in the country. Finally I was smart enough to ask why.

In a quivering little voice, he explained, "Mom, the song says 'Santa Claus is coming to town'. It doesn't say he'll come to the country!"

Needless to say, that was the year our family started singing "Santa Claus is coming to the country!" at the top of our lungs to drown out the original version each time we heard the song.

That, too, was the year we started the custom of leaving a bale of hay in our yard near the house. As we did, we went into great detail about how much Santa appreciated the farmers who left hay for his reindeer to eat while he filled the stockings and put the gifts under the tree.

Amy Jo and Johnathan were delighted with the idea that their hay would feed flying reindeer. And when they found only a little bit of it left, stomped into the snow, on Christmas morning, they squealed with delight.

This Christmas we're again looking forward to feeding the reindeer. I'm sure that it will be a Christmas custom in our family for many years to come...and that the lyrics, "Santa Claus is coming to the *country*" will stick in our minds the rest of our lives.

BRUNCH IS BECKONING! Jingle Bread, Ham a la King with Corn Custard, Hot Fruit Salad (recipes on opposite page).

HOLIDAY BRUNCH

Christmas is coming...and so is company!
Serve these festive favorites at your next gathering.

* * *

HOT FRUIT SALAD

Mrs. Charles Gorsh, North English, Iowa
(PICTURED ON OPPOSITE PAGE)

This is a perfect recipe to make in advance. It can be assembled the day before and baked the next morning!

> 1 can (29 ounces) pear halves, drained
> 1 can (29 ounces) peach halves, drained
> 1 can (30 ounces) apricot halves, drained
> 1 can (20 ounces) sliced pineapple, drained
> Red maraschino cherries, drained
> 1/2 cup butter *or* margarine
> 1/2 cup packed brown sugar
> 1 tablespoon cornstarch
> 1/2 to 1 teaspoon curry powder

Arrange pears, peaches, apricots and pineapple in a 9-in. x 9-in. baking pan. Decorate with cherries. In a saucepan, combine all remaining ingredients. Cook and stir over medium heat until thick and bubbly. Pour over fruit. Bake at 300° for 1 hour. Cool 30 minutes before serving. **Yield:** 9-12 servings.

* * *

JINGLE BREAD

Alice Kuiper, Racine, Wisconsin
(PICTURED ON OPPOSITE PAGE)

This recipe was served at my eldest daughter's wedding shower about 25 years ago by her girlfriend's mother. I've prepared it for special occasions ever since, and the bread is most enjoyable during the holidays.

> 2 cakes (5/8 ounce *each*) or 2/3 of a 2-ounce cake
>   compressed yeast
> 1/4 cup warm water (80°-90°)
> 2 teaspoons salt
> 1/3 cup sugar
> 1/4 cup shortening, melted
> 1 cup buttermilk *or* sour milk
> 2 eggs, beaten
> 4 to 4-1/2 cups all-purpose flour
> FILLING:
> 3/4 cup chopped nuts *or* raisins
> 1/2 of an 8-ounce can almond paste, crumbled
> 1/2 cup sugar
> 1 teaspoon ground cinnamon

THE CUTTING EDGE. When preparing Jingle Bread or similar filled breads or rolls, use dental floss to cut the dough. That way you won't ruin the shape and lose the filling.

> 2 tablespoons orange juice
> 2 tablespoons lemon juice

Confectioners' sugar icing, optional

Dissolve yeast in water. Set aside. In a large mixing bowl, combine salt, sugar, shortening and milk. Stir in eggs, yeast mixture and enough flour to form a moderately stiff dough. Place in a greased bowl, turning once to grease top. Cover and let rise in a warm place until doubled, about 1 hour. Meanwhile, for filling, combine nuts or raisins, almond paste, sugar, cinnamon, orange and lemon juice. Punch dough down. Roll out to an 18-in. x 14-in. rectangle. Spread with filling. Roll up, jelly roll-style, starting with the short side. Cut into 1-in. slices. Arrange in two layers in the bottom of a greased 10-in. tube pan. Cover and allow to rise until almost doubled, about 30-45 minutes. Bake at 350° for 40 minutes or until golden brown. Remove from the pan and allow to cool, right side up, on a wire rack. Frost with a light confectioners' sugar icing if desired. **Yield:** 16 servings.

* * *

HAM A LA KING WITH CORN CUSTARD

Mary Beth Jung, Grafton, Wisconsin
(PICTURED ON OPPOSITE PAGE)

I like to serve this at the holidays using leftover ham from one of our dinners. Our family especially likes the corn custard as the base for this hearty yet festive brunch.

CORN CUSTARD:
> 4 eggs, lightly beaten
> 2 cups cooked rice
> 1 can (17 ounces) whole kernel corn, drained
> 2 teaspoons sugar
> 1 teaspoon salt
> 1 cup milk, warmed

CREAMED HAM:
> 1/4 cup butter *or* margarine
> 1/2 pound fresh mushrooms, sliced
> 4 tablespoons all-purpose flour
> 1/2 teaspoon salt
> 1/8 teaspoon turmeric
> 1 can (10-1/2 ounces) chicken broth
> 1-1/4 cups milk
> 1 jar (2 ounces) chopped pimiento, drained
> 3 cups cubed cooked ham

Combine all corn custard ingredients. Pour into a greased 8-in. x 8-in. baking pan. Set in a large pan of hot water. Bake at 350° for 45 minutes or until firm. Meanwhile, for creamed ham, melt butter over medium heat in a large skillet. Saute mushrooms until tender. Add flour, salt and turmeric; blend well. Gradually stir in broth and milk. Cook and stir until thickened. Add pimiento and ham. Heat through. Serve over warm squares of corn custard. **Yield:** 8 servings.

HOT CHICKEN SALAD
Nayna Peterson, Genoa, Illinois

My aunt discovered this recipe, and it has become a family favorite. When taken to church or family get-togethers, the dish is sure to come home clean!

        3 cups cubed cooked chicken
        1 cup diced celery
        1 can (8 ounces) sliced water chestnuts, drained
        1 jar (2 ounces) chopped pimiento, drained
        1/2 cup toasted croutons
        1/2 teaspoon salt
        1/2 cup toasted sliced almonds
        3/4 cup mayonnaise
        3/4 cup sour cream
        2 tablespoons lemon juice
        2 teaspoons grated onion
TOPPING:
        1/2 cup buttered bread crumbs
        1/4 cup grated Parmesan cheese

In a large bowl, combine all ingredients except topping. Spoon into a greased 2-qt. casserole. Combine topping ingredients and sprinkle over casserole. Bake, uncovered, at 350° for 25-30 minutes or until topping is golden and dish is heated through. **Yield:** 8 servings.

CRANBERRY MARMALADE
Beverly Mix, Missoula, Montana

This recipe has been in our family for years. We especially like it on hot biscuits, dinner rolls or buttermilk muffins. It really has a great, zingy flavor!

        4 cups fresh *or* frozen cranberries
1-1/4 cups orange juice
        4 teaspoons grated orange peel
        1 cup sugar

In a saucepan, combine all ingredients. Bring to a boil. Reduce heat; simmer for 20-30 minutes, stirring occasionally. Refrigerate. **Yield:** 3 cups.

CRANBERRY/ORANGE PANCAKES
Mary Hanna, Maple Valley, Washington

My husband, our two children and I love to eat pancakes, so I try to add different fruits and grains to keep them interesting. I came up with this holiday recipe last winter and we all love it!

1-1/2 cups fresh *or* frozen cranberries
        2 tablespoons sugar *or* to taste
        1/2 cup cornmeal
        2 cups buttermilk baking mix
1-1/4 cups orange juice
        1 egg
Syrup

In a saucepan, combine cranberries and sugar. Cook over medium-high heat until cranberries pop. Cool. In a mixing bowl, combine remaining ingredients except syrup. Stir in cranberries. Pour batter by 1/4 cupfuls onto a lightly greased and preheated griddle or heavy skillet. Cook until golden brown, turning when top looks dry and bubbles form. Serve immediately with syrup. **Yield:** about 18 pancakes.

CHERRY MUFFINS
Donna Hofmann, Reedsburg, Wisconsin

We run the Parkview Bed & Breakfast, and I use cherries from my mother's cherry tree to make these festive-looking muffins for our guests.

        2 cups plus 2 tablespoons all-purpose flour
        1 cup sugar
        2 teaspoons baking powder
        1/4 teaspoon salt
        2 eggs, beaten
        1/2 cup milk
        1/2 cup butter *or* margarine, melted
        1 teaspoon almond extract
        2 cups fresh, frozen *or* canned pitted tart red
          cherries, drained
TOPPING:
        1 to 2 tablespoons sugar
        1/4 teaspoon ground nutmeg
        1 to 2 tablespoons sliced almonds

In a mixing bowl, stir together flour, sugar, baking powder and salt. Make a well in the center and set aside. In another bowl, combine eggs, milk, butter and extract. Add to flour mixture all at once; stir just until moistened. Gently fold in cherries. Spoon into well-greased muffin tins. Combine topping ingredients and sprinkle over batter. Bake at 375° for 20-25 minutes or until golden brown. Cool a few minutes before removing from pan. **Yield:** 12 muffins.

DANISH FRUIT SOUP
Virginia Hedrick, Kerens, West Virginia

This is a very old recipe which I've altered many times. It's a delightful brunch item, and keeps well in the refrigerator for several weeks.

        1 pound dried mixed fruit
        7 cups water
        1/2 cup raisins
        1 can (8 ounces) crushed pineapple, undrained
        1/4 teaspoon salt
        2 whole cloves
        1 stick cinnamon
        3/4 to 1 cup sugar
        1/4 cup quick-cooking tapioca
        2 tablespoons lemon juice
Sour cream *or* yogurt

In a saucepan, soak fruit and water for 1 hour. Stir in raisins, pineapple, salt and spices that have been tied into a cheesecloth bag. Simmer 1 hour. Discard spice bag. In a small bowl, combine sugar, tapioca and lemon juice; let stand 5 minutes. Stir into cooked fruit. Bring to a slow boil. Remove from heat; cover and allow to cool. Refrigerate, covered, until thoroughly chilled. Serve cold, garnished with a dollop of sour cream or yogurt. **Yield:** about 8 servings.

APPETIZERS & BEVERAGES

Delight friends and loved ones with a festive array of goodies to nibble on and enjoy.

* * *

ORANGE SPICED NUTS

Pamela Kinney, Irving, Texas

My husband is a pastor, so we often have large groups of people visiting our home. Cooking is a hobby for me, and this recipe not only tastes good, it fills the house with a wonderful aroma!

- 3 cups pecan halves
- 1 cup sugar
- 1/3 cup orange juice
- 1 tablespoon ground cinnamon
- 1/2 teaspoon salt
- 1/2 teaspoon ground cloves

Spread pecans on a jelly roll pan. Toast at 275° for 10 minutes. Remove from the oven and set aside. In a saucepan, combine sugar, orange juice, cinnamon, salt and cloves. Cook and stir over medium heat to the soft-ball stage (236°). Remove from the heat. Stir in nuts. Using a slotted spoon, remove nuts and spread on waxed paper. Separate and let dry 2 hours. Store in an airtight container. **Yield:** about 3 cups.

* * *

CRANBERRY/APPLE PUNCH

Betty Hollenback, Chesaning, Michigan
(PICTURED AT RIGHT)

I went to a party about 15 years ago and loved the punch. I asked for the recipe and have been serving it—with few variations—at all my parties ever since!

- 2 quarts water
- 2 cups sugar
- 1 can (16 ounces) frozen orange juice concentrate, thawed
- 1 can (12 ounces) frozen lemonade concentrate, thawed
- 2 quarts cranberry juice
- 1 quart apple juice
- 2 cups prepared tea, cooled

Orange, lemon and lime slices

In a large saucepan, heat water and sugar until dissolved. Cool. In a large punch bowl, combine sugar mixture with remaining ingredients except orange, lemon and lime slices, which are used for garnish. Chill with an ice ring. **Yield:** about 36 servings (6-1/2 quarts).

CHRISTMAS COMBO.
Celebrate the holidays with Deviled Ham and Cheese Ball and Cranberry/Apple Punch.

* * *

HOT CRAB DIP

Karen Buchholz, Sitka, Alaska

Serve this special dip at your next gathering and be prepared to hand out the recipe!

- 2 cans (6 ounces *each*) flaked crab, drained
- 2 packages (8 ounces *each*) cream cheese, softened
- 1/2 small onion, diced
- 1 tablespoon horseradish
- 2 dashes Worcestershire sauce
- 1/2 teaspoon salt
- 1/4 teaspoon pepper
- 1/3 cup slivered almonds

Assorted crackers

In a mixing bowl, combine all ingredients except last two. Spread in a 1-qt. baking dish. Sprinkle with almonds. Bake at 350° for 10-15 minutes or until mixture begins to bubble. Serve with crackers. **Yield:** 6-8 appetizer servings.

* * *

DEVILED HAM AND CHEESE BALL

Janice Fort, Houston, Minnesota
(PICTURED BELOW)

This flavorful appetizer is a crowd-pleaser at Christmastime. It's become a favorite of my husband's anytime.

- 1 package (8 ounces) cream cheese, softened
- 1 can (4-1/4 ounces) deviled ham
- 1 teaspoon prepared mustard
- 2 cups (8 ounces) shredded cheddar cheese
- 2 tablespoons chopped fresh chives *or* 2 teaspoons dried chives
- 1/2 cup chopped walnuts
- 1/4 cup snipped fresh parsley

Assorted crackers

In a small bowl, whip cream cheese, ham and mustard. Stir in cheddar cheese and chives. Shape into a ball, chilling beforehand if necessary. Roll in nuts and parsley. Wrap in plastic wrap and chill. Serve with assorted crackers. **Yield:** 2 cups.

FIT FOR A KING! Clockwise from top right: Mandarin Orange Cheesecake (p. 17), Aunt Maude's Fruitcake (p. 16), Honey and Spice Cornish Hens (p. 16), Cranberry Broccoli Salad (p. 17), Refrigerator Bran Cloverleaf Rolls (p. 16), Salmon Chowder (p. 17).

CHRISTMAS DINNER

Cook up a holiday feast that family and friends will not soon forget...using these festive recipes.

✳ ✳ ✳

AUNT MAUDE'S FRUITCAKE

Joyce Rupnow, Rock City, Illinois
(PICTURED ON PAGE 15)

My happiest childhood memories center around time spent with my grandparents and relatives in Tennessee. Often my Aunt Maude would visit from Mississippi with this pecan-filled fruitcake. It's equally delicious at a mountain picnic or a Christmas celebration!

>   4 eggs
>   1 cup sugar
>   2 cups all-purpose flour, *divided*
>   2 teaspoons baking powder
>   1/4 teaspoon salt
>   1 pound candied red cherries, halved
>   1 pound candied pineapple, cut into small pieces
>   1 pound pitted dates, cut into thirds
>   2 pounds shelled pecans, whole and broken pieces
>   1/2 cup light corn syrup
>   1 teaspoon water

Grease and line bottom and sides of two 9-in. x 5-in. x 3-in. loaf pans with waxed paper; set aside. In a mixing bowl, beat eggs with sugar; add 1 cup of flour, baking powder and salt; mix well. Set aside. In a large mixing bowl, coat the fruit with remaining cup of flour; add the batter, mixing slightly, then add pecans. Mix well until all pieces are coated with batter. Pour into prepared pans. Pack down firmly to eliminate air spaces. Bake at 275° for 2 hours. Cool 10-15 minutes in pans, then remove to wire racks. Peel off remaining waxed paper. Meanwhile in a saucepan, bring the corn syrup and water to a rolling boil. Brush immediately over warm fruitcakes. Cool completely before wrapping or storing. May be frozen. **Yield:** 2 loaves.

✳ ✳ ✳

REFRIGERATOR BRAN CLOVERLEAF ROLLS

June Lamey, Frelighsburg, Quebec
(PICTURED ON PAGE 14)

This is a very old recipe and was a favorite recipe of my mother's. The rolls have a unique flavor and are nutritious, too.

>   2 tablespoons shortening
>   2 cups water, *divided*
>   1/2 cup plus 1 tablespoon sugar, *divided*
>   1 cup all-bran cereal
>   1-1/2 teaspoons salt
>   2 packages (1/4 ounce *each*) active dry yeast
>   2 eggs, well-beaten
>   6 cups all-purpose flour
>   Melted butter

In a mixing bowl, combine shortening, 1 cup boiling water,

1/2 cup sugar, bran and salt. Stir until shortening dissolves. Cool. Dissolve yeast and remaining 1 tablespoon sugar in remaining 1 cup water that has been heated to 110°-115°. Let stand 5 minutes. Add to bran mixture. Stir in eggs and flour. Mix well. Place in a greased bowl. Cover and place in the refrigerator overnight. Shape each roll by making three 1-in. balls and placing them in a greased muffin tin; cover and let rise in a warm place until doubled, about 2-1/2 hours. Bake at 350° for 20 minutes or until light golden brown. Remove from the tins. Brush with melted butter and serve immediately. **Yield:** about 36 rolls.

✳ ✳ ✳

HONEY AND SPICE CORNISH HENS

Lynette Brewer, Fort Wayne, Indiana
(PICTURED ON PAGE 15)

We cooked 48 cornish hens at one time for a church dinner. As always, they turned out beautifully browned and delicious. The golden-colored stuffing is excellent.

>   4 Cornish game hens (1-1/2 pounds each)

STUFFING:
>   2/3 cup long grain rice
>   2 teaspoons instant chicken bouillon granules
>   2 teaspoons lemon juice
>   1/4 teaspoon ground turmeric
>   1/4 teaspoon ground cinnamon
>   Dash of ground cloves
>   Dash of pepper
>   2 cups water
>   2 tablespoons honey
>   2 tablespoons butter
>   1/2 cup light raisins
>   1/4 cup chopped walnuts
>   1/2 teaspoon salt
>   Cooking oil

BASTING SAUCE:
>   1/4 cup lemon juice
>   2 tablespoons butter *or* margarine, melted

In a saucepan, combine the rice, bouillon, lemon juice, turmeric, cinnamon, cloves and pepper. Stir in water and bring to a boil. Reduce heat; cover and simmer about 25 minutes or until liquid is absorbed; remove from heat. Stir in honey, butter, raisins and nuts. Season cavities of hens with salt; lightly stuff with rice mixture; fasten necks closed with toothpicks. Place hens breast side up in a shallow roasting pan. Brush with oil, cover loosely with foil and bake at 375° for 30 minutes. For basting sauce, combine lemon juice and butter. Remove foil and discard; baste hens with lemon butter. Return hens to oven and bake, about 45 minutes longer, basting every 15 minutes, or until done. **Yield:** 4 servings.

❋ ❋ ❋

SALMON CHOWDER

Donald Clair, Dallas, Oregon
(PICTURED ON PAGE 14)

Salmon has a wonderful flavor that comes through in this chowder recipe I developed. It's a nice change of pace for a holiday dish.

      6 slices bacon, diced
1-1/2 cups diced celery
      1 cup chopped onion
      3 cups diced peeled potatoes
      2 cans (14-1/2 ounces *each*) chicken broth
1-1/2 teaspoons salt
   1/2 teaspoon paprika
   1/2 teaspoon dried thyme *or* dried dill weed
   1/4 teaspoon pepper
      2 large salmon steaks, cooked, boned and flaked
         or 1 can (15 ounces) salmon, drained, boned
         and flaked
      3 tablespoons all-purpose flour
      2 cups milk, *divided*
      1 cup cream

In a Dutch oven, partially cook bacon. Add celery, onion and potatoes. Cook, stirring occasionally, until tender. Add chicken broth, salt, paprika, thyme or dill and pepper. Bring to a boil. Reduce heat, add salmon and simmer 15 minutes. Blend flour into 1/4 cup milk to make a paste. Pour remaining milk and cream into Dutch oven. Quickly stir in the flour mixture. Cook, stirring frequently, until heated through and lightly thickened, about 15 minutes. **Yield:** about 3 quarts.

❋ ❋ ❋

MANDARIN ORANGE CHEESECAKE

Shirley Connolley, Berwyn, Alberta
(PICTURED ON PAGE 15)

This cheesecake is super for a special occasion like Christmas dinner. I found it in an old cookbook and the family loves it.

CRUST:
1-3/4 cups graham cracker crumbs
   1/2 cup butter, melted
      1 tablespoon sugar
   1/2 teaspoon ground cinnamon

FILLING:
      2 packages (8 ounces *each*) cream cheese, softened
      2 eggs
   3/4 cup sugar, *divided*
      1 teaspoon vanilla extract
      2 cups (16 ounces) sour cream
      2 cans (11 ounces *each*) mandarin oranges, drained

GLAZE:
   1/3 cup orange juice
   1/4 cup sugar
1-1/2 teaspoons cornstarch

Combine crust ingredients. Press into the bottom and sides of a 9-in. springform pan. Bake at 350° for 5 minutes; cool. Set aside. For filling, beat cream cheese, eggs, 1/2 cup sugar and vanilla until fluffy. Pour into the crust. Bake at 350° for 30 min-

utes. Meanwhile, in a small bowl, stir together remaining sugar and sour cream. Spoon over top of cake; bake 15 minutes longer; cool. For glaze, combine juice, sugar and cornstarch in a saucepan. Cook over medium heat until clear, stirring constantly. Cool. Arrange orange slices on top of cheesecake, spoon glaze over fruit. **Yield:** 12 servings.

❋ ❋ ❋

SQUASH AND APPLE BAKE

Gloria Onderdonk, Greenland, New Hampshire

We have a lot of squash and apples in New Hampshire, and this recipe is a delightful holiday dish. My husband urged me to send it.

      2 pounds butternut *or* buttercup squash, peeled,
         seeded and cut into 1/2-inch pieces
      2 baking apples, cored and cut into 1/2-inch slices
   1/2 cup packed brown sugar
   1/4 cup butter *or* margarine, melted
      1 tablespoon all-purpose flour
   1/2 teaspoon salt
   1/2 teaspoon mace

Arrange squash in ungreased 12-in. x 8-in. baking dish; top with apple slices. Combine remaining ingredients; spoon over apples. Bake at 350° for 50-60 minutes or until squash and apples are tender. **Yield:** 4-6 servings.

❋ ❋ ❋

CRANBERRY BROCCOLI SALAD

Shirley Leighton, Randolph, Massachusetts
(PICTURED ON PAGE 14)

I first tried this salad at a friend's house, and it has been a favorite at my festive gatherings ever since.

1-1/4 cups fresh *or* frozen cranberries, halved
      2 cups broccoli florets
      4 cups shredded cabbage
      1 cup coarsely chopped walnuts
   1/2 cup raisins
      1 small onion, finely minced
      8 slices bacon, cooked and crumbled
      1 cup mayonnaise
   1/3 cup sugar
      2 tablespoons cider vinegar

In a large bowl, combine cranberries, broccoli, cabbage, walnuts, raisins, onion and bacon. Combine remaining ingredients and pour over cranberry mixture. Toss well. Cover and refrigerate for up to 24 hours. **Yield:** 6-8 servings.

FESTIVE PHONING. Before you begin baking sticky items, place a plastic bag near the phone. Why? If someone calls while your hands are doughy or greasy, you can just slip your hand into the bag and answer quickly!

ICE CREAM PUMPKIN PIE

Celeste Borges, Kailua-Kona, Hawaii

I'm delighted when people enjoy eating my goodies—and this recipe is one that everyone enjoys. It was given to me by a friend years ago and is a pleasant, refreshing treat.

  1 can (16 ounces) pumpkin
  1 can (14 ounces) sweetened condensed milk
  1 teaspoon ground cinnamon
  1/2 teaspoon ground ginger
  1/2 teaspoon ground nutmeg
  1/2 teaspoon salt
  1 pint butter pecan ice cream, softened
  1 graham cracker crust (10 inches), baked and
      cooled
Whipped cream
Chopped nuts

In a mixing bowl, combine first six ingredients; beat well. Stir in ice cream. Spoon into crust. Freeze several hours or overnight. Let pie stand at room temperature for 10 minutes before serving. Garnish with whipped cream and nuts. **Yield:** 8 servings.

HOLIDAY SHORTCAKE

Jennifer Whitaker, Winchendon, Massachusetts

Perfect for Christmastime, this colorful recipe calls for cranberries, but its surprising flavor makes it more like a mock strawberry shortcake.

  1 cup fresh *or* frozen cranberries
  1 apple, cored and peeled
  1 can (8 ounces) crushed pineapple, undrained
  1 cup sugar
  6 baking powder biscuits
Whipped cream

In a food processor, finely chop cranberries and apple. In a mixing bowl, combine chopped fruit with pineapple and sugar; mix well. Chill. Serve on split biscuits with a dollop of whipped cream. **Yield:** 6 servings.

CRANBERRY ARCTIC FROST SALAD

Lisa R. Hurliman, Cloverdale, Oregon

I took this to a potluck dinner at my in-laws the first Christmas of our marriage, but with all the excitement, we almost forgot to take it out of the freezer! It ended up being served after the pumpkin pie, yet everyone enjoyed it and none of it went to waste.

  1 cup heavy cream
  1 cup chopped nuts
  1 can (20 ounces) crushed pineapple, drained
  1 can (16 ounces) whole-berry cranberry sauce
  2 tablespoons mayonnaise
  2 tablespoons sugar
  1 package (8 ounces) cream cheese, softened

In a large mixing bowl, whip cream. Fold in nuts and pineap-

ple; set aside. In a food processor or blender, liquify cranberries; add mayonnaise, sugar and cream cheese; blend together. Fold cranberry mixture into cream mixture; pour into a 12-in. x 7-1/2-in. x 2-in. baking dish. Freeze. About 15 minutes before serving, remove from freezer; slice and serve. **Yield:** 12 servings.

PRIME RIB ROAST WITH MUSTARD CRUMB CRUST

Nancy Hillegass, Berlin, Pennsylvania

I discovered this recipe several years ago and served it to family that Christmas Eve. It was a big hit and has been ever since.

  1 prime beef rib roast, 3 to 4 ribs (about 8
      pounds), trimmed
  8 slices firm white bread, coarsely crumbled
  1/2 cup chopped fresh parsley
  1/3 cup Dijon mustard
  1/3 cup mayonnaise
  1/4 cup grated Parmesan cheese
  2 tablespoons lemon juice
  2 garlic cloves, crushed
  1/2 teaspoon salt
  1/2 teaspoon dried thyme
  1/2 teaspoon dried basil
  1/4 teaspoon freshly ground pepper
Fresh herb sprigs, optional

In a large roasting pan, place roast, fat side up. Roast meat about 2 hours or until meat thermometer registers 120°. Meanwhile, in a medium bowl, combine remaining ingredients; blend well. Remove roast from oven; spread stuffing mixture over the fat side of the roast. Return roast to the oven, bake until stuffing is browned and meat reaches desired degree of doneness, 140° for rare, 160° for medium, 170° for well done. If stuffing becomes too brown, cover loosely with foil. Remove roast from pan, and place on a serving platter. Cover loosely with foil and let stand for 15 minutes before carving. Garnish with fresh herb sprigs if desired. **Yield:** 12-16 servings.

OVEN HASH BROWN POTATOES

Virginia Dane, Twin Falls, Idaho

People are apt to come running when they smell the aroma of these succulent hash browns baking in the oven.

  2 pounds frozen hash brown potatoes, thawed
  1/4 cup chopped onions, optional
  2 cups (16 ounces) sour cream
  1 can (10-3/4 ounces) cream of chicken soup,
      undiluted
1-1/2 cups shredded cheddar cheese
  1 teaspoon salt
  1/4 teaspoon pepper
  2 cups crushed potato chips
  1/4 cup butter *or* margarine, melted

In a large mixing bowl, combine first 7 ingredients. Spread into a greased 9-in. x 13-in. baking dish. Combine potato chips and butter; spread over potatoes. Bake, covered, at 350° for 45 minutes. **Yield:** 12-15 servings.

* * *

COFFEE GATEAU

Eileen VanRyke, Manhattan, Montana

I entered this oh-so-good recipe in our local fair and won a ribbon. It's a well-liked cake by family and friends.

1/2 cup plus 2 tablespoons butter, softened
1 cup sugar, *divided*
6 eggs, *separated*
5 ounces semisweet chocolate, melted
1 cup all-purpose flour
1/4 teaspoon baking powder
1/8 teaspoon salt
1/4 teaspoon ground cinnamon

COFFEE ICING:
1/3 cup cornstarch
1 to 2 tablespoons instant coffee granules
1 cup sugar
1-3/4 cups milk
1-1/2 cups butter
Chocolate shavings

In a mixing bowl, cream together butter and 1/2 cup sugar until fluffy. Add egg yolks, one at a time, beating well after each addition. Stir in chocolate. Sift together flour, baking powder, salt and cinnamon; add to creamed mixture. In another bowl, beat egg whites until stiff; beat in remaining sugar. Gently fold into the butter mixture. Pour into a greased 9-in. springform pan. Bake at 375° for 50-60 minutes. Do not overbake. Cool on a wire rack. Meanwhile, in a saucepan, combine the cornstarch, coffee and sugar. Add milk, stirring until dry ingredients are dissolved. Cook over medium heat until mixture thickens, stirring constantly. Remove from the heat, cover mixture with plastic wrap and cool completely, stirring frequently to prevent lumps. In a mixing bowl, cream butter; gradually add coffee mixture, beating well after each addition. Split cake into 3 layers. Spread icing between layers and over the top and sides of cake. Garnish with chocolate shavings. **Yield:** 16 servings.

* * *

ROAST DUCK WITH TANGERINE SAUCE

Crystal Southwood, Bakersfield, California

This is one of the best main dishes you'll ever make. I even use the sauce occasionally on turkey. It's delicious and my husband—who has been known at other times to ask "What's burning?"—loves it!

1 domestic duckling (3 to 5 pounds), neck and giblets reserved
Salt
Pepper
4 small yams
2 cups water
1 large onion, quartered
1 bay leaf
2 tablespoons cornstarch
1-1/2 cups fresh tangerine juice, *divided*
3 tablespoons slivered tangerine peel
3 tablespoons honey

Season cavity of the duck with salt and pepper; place breast side

down on a rack in roasting pan. Bake at 325°, uncovered, for 1 hour, removing excess fat from pan during baking. Remove from oven, turn duck breast side up; add yams; baste duck and yams with drippings. Return to oven and bake about 1 hour longer or until duck and yams are tender, basting the duck and turning the yams every 15 minutes. Meanwhile, in a 2-qt. saucepan, combine water, onion, bay leaf and reserved neck and giblets. Cover and simmer 1 hour. Strain stock; return to pan and reduce to about 1/2 cup. Remove duck and yams from the pan; keep warm. Skim fat from drippings; reserve 2 tablespoons for sauce. Combine cornstarch with 2 tablespoons tangerine juice; add to roasting pan with remaining juice, stock, peel and honey. Boil over high heat, stirring until sauce thickens and clears, about 2 minutes. Season to taste with salt and pepper. To serve, arrange duck and yams on warmed platter; spoon sauce over duck. **Yield:** 4 servings.

* * *

HOOSIER BAKED RICE

Phyllis Fulmer, Greenfield, Indiana

This rice recipe is great with chicken, turkey or simply alone with salad and warm rolls. Even holiday dinner guests who didn't like rice before quickly convert.

1 cup long grain brown rice
2 cans (10-1/2 ounces *each***) chicken broth**
6 slices bacon, cut into 1-inch pieces
1 cup chopped onion
2 small carrots, diced
8 ounces fresh mushrooms, sliced
1/4 teaspoon dried thyme
1/4 teaspoon dried marjoram
1/8 teaspoon pepper

In a saucepan, combine rice and chicken broth. Bring to a boil, reduce heat and simmer, covered, 40-50 minutes or until rice is tender. Do not drain. Meanwhile, in a skillet, lightly fry bacon; drain all but 2 tablespoons of drippings. Stir in remaining ingredients and lightly saute until onions are soft. Combine rice and onion mixture in a greased 2-qt. baking dish. Bake at 350°, covered, for 35-40 minutes. Let stand about 5 minutes before serving. **Yield:** 6-8 servings.

* * *

RED CABBAGE

Phyllis Huff, Longview, Washington

My mother-in-law gave me this recipe many years ago. It's still a favorite.

1/4 cup butter *or* **margarine**
8 cups shredded red cabbage
1 large onion, chopped
1/2 cup packed brown sugar
1/2 cup vinegar
2 to 3 teaspoons salt
1/2 teaspoon ground cloves
1/8 teaspoon pepper

In a large saucepan, melt butter. Add remaining ingredients and cook over low heat, covered, stirring occasionally, 30 minutes. **Yield:** 8-10 servings.

FESTIVE BREADS. *Clockwise from left:*
Orange Butter Coffee Cake (p. 23), Pumpkin Apple
Streusel Muffins (p. 24), Caramel Pecan Rolls (p. 23),
Cherry Pecan Bread (p. 24), Holiday Wreaths (p. 23),
Lemon Bread (p. 22), Christmas Tree Bread (p. 22).

CHRISTMAS BREADS

Served warm from the oven or wrapped with ribbons,
these breads hark back to Christmas kitchens of old.

✳ ✳ ✳

LEMON BREAD

Judy Watkins, Hartford, Iowa
(PICTURED ON PAGE 20)

This bread has a nice fresh flavor and is good for gifts.

1-3/4 cups all-purpose flour
  3/4 cup sugar
    2 teaspoons baking powder
    2 teaspoons finely shredded lemon peel
  1/2 teaspoon salt
    1 egg
  3/4 cup milk
  1/4 cup vegetable oil
    1 tablespoon lemon juice

In a mixing bowl, stir together first five ingredients; set aside. In another bowl, beat together egg, milk, oil and lemon juice. Add to dry ingredients, stirring just until moistened. Pour batter into two greased 6-in. x 3-in. x 2-in. loaf pans. Bake at 350° for 35-40 minutes or until breads test done. Cool in pans 10 minutes. Remove from pans; cool thoroughly on a wire rack. **Yield:** 2 loaves.

✳ ✳ ✳

CHRISTMAS TREE BREAD

Flo Burtnett, Gage, Oklahoma
(PICTURED ON PAGE 20)

This decorative bread recipe is a standard size—just right for your holiday table!

    1 package (1/4 ounce) active dry yeast
  1/4 cup warm water (110°-115°)
  3/4 cup milk
  1/4 cup shortening
  1/4 cup sugar
    1 teaspoon salt
    1 egg, beaten
    3 to 3-1/2 cups all-purpose flour
GLAZE:
    2 tablespoons milk
  1/2 teaspoon vanilla extract
    1 cup sifted confectioners' sugar

Red and green candied cherries

In a mixing bowl, dissolve yeast in water. Let stand 5 minutes. In a saucepan, combine milk, shortening, sugar and salt; cook over medium heat until mixture reaches 110°-115°. Add milk mixture, egg and 1 cup of flour to yeast mixture; beat until well blended. Gradually stir in enough remaining flour to make a slightly stiff dough. Turn dough onto a floured surface; knead until smooth and elastic, about 6-8 minutes. Place in a greased bowl, turning to grease top. Cover and let rise in a warm place until doubled, about 1 hour. Punch down and divide in half; shape each half into 23 balls. On a large, greased, waxed paper-lined baking sheet, arrange 21 balls in a triangular shape, about 1/4-in. apart, in rows of 6, 5, 4, 3, 2 and 1. To form the tree trunk, center 2 balls at the base. Repeat procedure with remaining dough to make another tree. Cover and let rise until doubled, about 30 minutes. Bake at 375° for 12-15 minutes or until golden brown. Cool slightly and transfer to a flat serving platter. For glaze, in a small bowl combine milk, vanilla and confectioners' sugar; drizzle over trees. Garnish with cherries. **Yield:** 2 breads.

✳ ✳ ✳

EMMA'S CHRISTMAS BRAIDS

Arlene M. Oliver, Waterloo, Iowa
(PICTURED ON COVER)

In the 1940's, a friend gave this Scandinavian recipe to my mother, who changed it by braiding and decorating each loaf. She's made dozens at Christmas, and our family is carrying on the tradition.

    1 cake (5/8 ounce) compressed yeast
  1/4 cup warm water (80°-90°)
1-1/2 cups milk, scalded
  1/4 cup butter
  3/8 cup sugar
    1 teaspoon salt
5-1/4 to 5-3/4 cups all-purpose flour
    1 egg, beaten
  1/4 teaspoon lemon extract
  1/4 teaspoon almond extract
    1 cup finely chopped mixed candied fruit
  1/4 cup dried currants
LEMON ICING:
    1 cup sifted confectioners' sugar
    1 to 2 tablespoons milk
  1/4 teaspoon lemon extract

Whole pecans and halved candied cherries for garnish, optional

In a small bowl, dissolve yeast in water. Let stand 5 minutes. In a mixing bowl, combine milk and butter; stir until butter melts. When mixture is lukewarm, add yeast mixture and sugar. Add salt and 2-1/2 cups of flour; beat well. Add egg and extracts; beat thoroughly. Stir in fruit, currants and enough remaining flour to form a stiff dough. Knead until smooth and elastic, about 6-8 minutes. Place in a greased bowl, turning once to grease top. Cover and let rise in a warm place until doubled, about 1-1/2 hours. Punch dough down and divide into thirds. Divide and shape each third into three ropes about 12-14 inches long. Place three ropes on a greased baking sheet, and braid loosely from center to ends. Repeat with remaining six ropes. Cover and let rise until doubled, about 30-40 minutes. Bake at 375° about 25 minutes or until golden brown; cool on a wire rack. For icing, combine ingredients and drizzle over breads. Garnish with pecans and cherries if desired. **Yield:** 3 breads.

***

CARAMEL PECAN ROLLS
Mrs. Vivian Bailey, Cedar Falls, Iowa
(PICTURED ON PAGE 21)

I usually double this recipe and share half of the rolls with my son and his family. He has five children and they can eat them in a hurry!

1 package (1/4 ounce) active dry yeast
1 cup warm water (110°-115°)
1/4 cup sugar
1 teaspoon salt
3-1/4 to 3-3/4 cups all-purpose flour, *divided*
1 egg
2 tablespoons butter *or* margarine, softened
TOPPING:
1/3 cup butter *or* margarine, melted
1/2 cup packed light brown sugar
1 tablespoon light corn syrup
1 tablespoon water
1 cup whole pecans
FILLING:
2 tablespoons butter *or* margarine, softened
1/3 cup sugar
1-1/2 teaspoons ground cinnamon

In a mixing bowl, dissolve yeast in water. Stir in sugar, salt and 1-1/2 cups flour; beat well. Beat in egg and butter. By hand, stir in enough flour to make a soft dough. Place in a greased bowl, turning once to grease top. Cover and refrigerate overnight. For topping, combine butter, sugar, corn syrup and water in a small saucepan; heat and stir until blended. Pour topping into a greased 13-in. x 9-in. x 2-in. baking pan. Sprinkle with pecans; set aside. Meanwhile, punch dough down. On a lightly floured surface, roll dough into a 15-in. x 12-in. rectangle; spread with butter. Combine sugar and cinnamon; sprinkle over dough. Starting with the shorter side, roll up tightly, pinching edges to seal. Cut into 12 slices. Place over topping in pan. Cover and let rise until almost doubled, about 1 hour. Bake at 375° for 20-25 minutes or until golden brown. Remove from oven. Invert immediately onto a baking sheet. **Yield:** 12 rolls.

***

HOLIDAY WREATHS
Jo Neyer, Mt. Pleasant, Michigan
(PICTURED ON PAGE 21)

I make at least half a dozen of these pretty breads each year to give as presents. They make a beautiful centerpiece on the dinner table, too.

5-1/2 to 6 cups all-purpose flour, *divided*
2 packages (1/4 ounce *each*) active dry yeast
1/2 cup sugar
1 teaspoon salt
1 teaspoon ground cardamom
1 cup milk
1/2 cup water
1/3 cup butter *or* margarine
2 eggs
1/2 cup chopped candied cherries
1/2 cup diced mixed candied fruit
Confectioners' sugar glaze, optional
Red and green candied cherries, optional

In a large mixing bowl, combine 2-1/2 cups flour, yeast, sugar, salt and cardamom; mix well. In a saucepan, heat milk, water and butter until warm (120°-130°); add to flour mixture. Stir in eggs. With an electric mixer, blend at low speed until moistened; beat 3 minutes at medium speed. By hand, gradually stir in the fruit and enough remaining flour to make a soft dough. Knead on a lightly floured surface until smooth and elastic, about 6-8 minutes. Place in a greased bowl, turning once to grease top. Cover and let rise in a warm place until doubled, about 1 hour. Punch dough down and divide in half. Divide each half into three pieces. On a lightly floured surface, roll each piece into a 24-in. rope. Place three ropes on a greased baking sheet, and braid loosely from center to ends. Form into a circle; pinch ends together to seal. Repeat with remaining three ropes. Cover and let rise until almost doubled, about 20-30 minutes. Bake at 350° for 20-25 minutes or until golden brown. Cool. If desired, drizzle with a confectioners' sugar glaze and garnish with red and green candied cherries. **Yield:** 2 breads.

***

ORANGE BUTTER COFFEE CAKE
Joyce Scott, Lincoln, Nebraska
(PICTURED ON PAGE 20)

I've prepared this for our family of six for many years. It's also a great treat for entertaining a group of friends during the holidays.

1 package (1/4 ounce) active dry yeast
1/4 cup warm water (110°-115°)
1 cup sugar, *divided*
1 teaspoon salt
2 eggs, beaten
1/2 cup sour cream
8 tablespoons (1/2 cup) butter *or* margarine, melted, *divided*
2-3/4 to 3 cups all-purpose flour
1 cup flaked coconut, toasted
2 tablespoons grated orange peel
ORANGE GLAZE:
1/2 cup sugar
1/3 cup sour cream
4 teaspoons orange juice
3 tablespoons butter *or* margarine

In a mixing bowl, dissolve yeast in warm water. Let stand 5 minutes. Stir in 1/4 cup sugar, salt, eggs, sour cream and 6 tablespoons butter. Gradually add enough flour to form a stiff dough, beating well after each addition. Place in a greased bowl, turning once to grease top. Cover and let rise in a warm place until doubled, about 1-1/2 hours. Meanwhile, combine remaining sugar, coconut and orange peel in a small bowl; set aside. Punch dough down. Knead on a well-floured surface about 15 times. Roll out half of the dough into a 12-in. circle. Brush with 1 tablespoon of remaining butter. Sprinkle with 1/2 cup of coconut mixture. Cut into 12 wedges. Roll up, starting with wide end and rolling to the point. Place rolls, point side down, in a well-greased 9-in. round or 13-in. x 9-in. x 2-in. baking pan. Repeat with remaining dough. Cover and let rise until doubled, about 30-45 minutes. Sprinkle rolls with remaining coconut mixture. Bake at 350° for 20-25 minutes or until golden brown; leave rolls in pan. For glaze, combine all ingredients in a small saucepan. Cook and stir over medium heat until boiling; pour glaze over hot rolls. Serve warm. **Yield:** 24 rolls.

PUMPKIN APPLE STREUSEL MUFFINS

Janet M. Washam, Langdon, New Hampshire
(PICTURED ON PAGE 20)

My grandmother, whose cooking advice and comments I value greatly, called these muffins delicious. So they must be!

2-1/2 cups all-purpose flour
    2 cups sugar
    1 tablespoon pumpkin pie spice
    1 teaspoon baking soda
    1/2 teaspoon salt
    2 eggs, lightly beaten
    1 cup pumpkin
    1/2 cup vegetable oil
    2 cups finely chopped peeled apples
STREUSEL:
    2 tablespoons all-purpose flour
    1/4 cup sugar
    1/2 teaspoon ground cinnamon
    4 teaspoons butter *or* margarine, softened

In a large bowl, combine first five ingredients; set aside. In another bowl, combine eggs, pumpkin and oil. Stir pumpkin mixture into dry ingredients just until moistened. Stir in apples. Spoon batter into greased muffin tins, filling 3/4 full. Combine streusel ingredients and sprinkle over batter. Bake at 400° for 20-22 minutes or until toothpick comes out clean. **Yield:** 2 dozen.

CHRISTMAS KRINGLE

Cathy Anusesky, Stillwater, New York

This recipe, given to me by a dear aunt, is convenient because it can be made ahead, frozen and reheated as needed. My husband and our two sons love this delicious kringle on Christmas morning.

    2 packages (1/4 ounce *each*) active dry yeast
    1/2 cup warm water (110°-115°)
    1/2 cup sugar, *divided*
    1/2 cup milk
    1 teaspoon salt
    1/2 cup butter *or* margarine
    2 eggs, beaten
    4 to 4-1/2 cups all-purpose flour
    1 can (12-1/2 ounces) almond filling
TOPPING:
    1 egg white
    1 teaspoon water
    3 teaspoons sugar
    3 tablespoons sliced almonds

In a small bowl, combine yeast, water and 1 teaspoon sugar; let stand 5 minutes. In a saucepan, heat milk, salt, butter and remaining sugar to 110°-115°. Cool. Stir in yeast mixture and eggs. Add 2 cups flour; beat until smooth. Add enough of the remaining flour to form a soft dough. Turn out onto a lightly floured surface; knead until smooth and elastic, about 6-8 minutes. Place in a greased bowl, turning once to grease top. Cover and let rise in a warm place until doubled, about 1-1/2 hours. Punch dough down and divide into thirds. On a lightly floured surface, roll each third into a 30-in. x 4-in. rectangle. Place 1/3

of the almond filling down the center of each strip. Fold edges over filling and pinch edges together. Place, seam side down, on three greased cookie sheets. Shape each into a large oval, pinching ends to join. Cover and let rise until doubled, about 30-45 minutes. Beat egg white lightly with water; brush over kringles. Sprinkle each with 1 teaspoon sugar and 1 tablespoon almonds. Bake at 350° for about 25 minutes or until golden brown. Remove to wire racks to cool. **Yield:** 3 kringles.

CHERRY PECAN BREAD

Pam Wyatt, Upton, Kentucky
(PICTURED ON PAGE 21)

The red and green cherries make this a very pretty Christmas bread.

    2 cups all-purpose flour
    3/4 cup sugar
    1 teaspoon baking soda
    1/2 teaspoon salt
    2 eggs, beaten
    1/2 cup vegetable oil
    1 cup buttermilk
    1 teaspoon vanilla extract
    1 cup chopped pecans
    1/2 cup red maraschino cherries, drained and quartered
    1/2 cup green maraschino cherries, drained and quartered

In a mixing bowl, stir together flour, sugar, soda and salt; set aside. In another bowl, combine eggs, oil, buttermilk and vanilla. Add to dry ingredients, stirring just until combined. Fold in nuts and cherries. Pour into a greased 9-in. x 5-in. x 3-in. loaf pan. Bake at 350° for 50-55 minutes or until the bread tests done. Cool in pan for 10 minutes; remove to wire rack. **Yield:** 1 loaf.

PUMPKIN BREAD

Debbie Jones, California, Maryland

This is my grandmother's recipe, and I've never seen it fail.

3-1/3 cups all-purpose flour
    2 teaspoons baking soda
    1 teaspoon ground cinnamon
    1 teaspoon ground nutmeg
    1/2 teaspoon salt
    1 cup vegetable oil
    3 cups sugar
    4 eggs
1-1/2 cups solid-pack pumpkin
    2/3 cup water
    2/3 cup chopped walnuts
    2/3 cup raisins

In a large mixing bowl, combine flour, baking soda, cinnamon, nutmeg and salt; set aside. In another bowl, place oil, sugar, eggs, pumpkin and water. Stir into flour mixture. Add nuts and raisins; mix together only until dry ingredients are moistened. Divide batter between two greased 9-in. x 5-in. x 3-in. loaf pans. Bake at 350° for 50-60 minutes or until breads test done. Cool for 10 minutes on wire rack before removing from pans. **Yield:** 2 loaves.

WRAP UP YOUR BAKING WITH CROSS-STITCH

IF YOU'RE making quick breads for holiday dinners this year (see pages 22-24 for recipes), try wrapping your loaves in these cheery cross-stitched cloths. Great for "gift loaves", too!

CROSS-STITCHED BREAD CLOTHS

Materials needed: No. 26 tapestry needle; charts; DMC six-strand floss in colors listed on color keys; 14-count Ivory Salem bread cloths*.

Directions: Separate six-strand floss and use two strands of floss for cross-stitches and for backstitches.

Use color key and chart to stitch design of choice. For placement of design, broad line indicates inside edge of fringe. Be sure to cross all stitches in same direction.

Do not knot floss at back of work. To start stitching, leave a short tail at back of work and hold in place. Work first few stitches around this tail to secure floss. End stitching by running floss under several stitches at back of work.

When the design is completed, fringe your finished piece by gently pulling threads on all sides to the machine-stitched line.

*To order Sal-em bread cloths, request a catalog from Carolina Cross Stitch Inc., P.O. Box 845, Laurinburg NC 28352.

Or you can make you own bread cloth by cutting 14-count Sal-em cloth or any even-weave fabric 18 in. x 18 in. To fringe, machine-stitch 1/2 in. from all raw edges and unravel fabric to machine-stitched lines. ❋

WARM WISHES COLOR KEY

		DMC
◣	Garnet	816
◆	Christmas Green	699
♥	Lt. Beige Gray	822

Backstitch the hearts with Christmas Green DMC 699.

HAPPY HOLIDAYS COLOR KEY

		DMC
◣	Garnet	816
★	Lt. Carnation	893

Backstitch greenery with Christmas Green DMC 699. Backstitch holly berries and area around bow with Garnet DMC 816.

DELIGHTFUL DISPLAY. Clockwise from bottom: Caramel Toffee Squares (p. 28), Orange/Walnut Shortbread (p. 28), Cocoa Nut Winners (p. 28), Chocolate-Orange Crunchies (p. 29), Gingerbread Cookies (p. 29), Pfefferneusse Cookies (p. 29), Swedish Cookies (p. 30), No-Bake Cherry Balls (p. 28).

COOKIES & CANDIES

Sweeten the holidays with these kitchen confections—
great for family, friends, guests and gifts!

※ ※ ※

COCOA NUT WINNERS

Joy Sappington, Wyandotte, Oklahoma
(PICTURED ON PAGE 26)

My mother made this recipe often at Christmas, and now I make it. It must be a "winner", because each time I serve it to guests they ask for the recipe. My farm husband and 3 children just ask for more cookies!

   1 cup butter
   2 cups packed brown sugar
   1 teaspoon vanilla extract
   2 eggs
   3 cups all-purpose flour
   1 teaspoon baking soda
1/2 teaspoon salt
   3 tablespoons unsweetened cocoa
   1 cup chopped nuts

In a mixing bowl, cream butter and sugar until smooth. Add remaining ingredients except nuts; mix until well blended. (Dough will be very stiff.) Stir in nuts. Using lightly floured waxed paper, shape into six 8-in. x 1-in. rolls. Chill overnight. Cut rolls into 1/4-in. slices. Place 2 in. apart on greased cookie sheets. Bake at 350° for 8-10 minutes or until firm to the touch. **Yield:** 13 dozen.

※ ※ ※

CARAMEL TOFFEE SQUARES

Mrs. Keith Snyder, Wallenstein, Ontario
(PICTURED ON PAGE 26)

When I have a mixture of cookies and squares on a plate, my husband and children always pick these out first.

CRUST:
   9 tablespoons butter *or* margarine
  1/4 cup sugar
1-1/4 cups all-purpose flour
FILLING:
  1/2 cup butter *or* margarine
  1/2 cup packed brown sugar
   2 tablespoons light corn syrup
  1/2 of a 14-ounce can sweetened condensed milk
   1 package (12 ounces) semisweet chocolate chips

In a mixing bowl, combine crust ingredients until crumbly. Firmly press into an ungreased 9-in. x 9-in. x 2-in. baking pan. Bake at 350° for 15 minutes or until edges are lightly browned. Cool. Meanwhile, in a saucepan, combine butter, sugar, corn syrup and milk. Bring to a boil over medium heat. Reduce heat; cook and stir until mixture reaches 234° (soft-ball stage). Remove from heat. Stir and pour over the crust. Melt chocolate chips in a saucepan over low heat. Pour over filling. Chill. Cut into 1-1/2-in. squares. **Yield:** 3 dozen.

※ ※ ※

ORANGE/WALNUT SHORTBREAD

Betty Harrison, McMinnville, Oregon
(PICTURED ON PAGE 26)

With grown children, I don't get as much opportunity to really cook up a storm. But during the holidays I do, and this shortbread—drizzled with orange glaze—always makes the menu. Serve it with coffee or tea.

1-1/4 cups all-purpose flour
  1/4 cup sugar
  1/8 teaspoon salt
   2 teaspoons grated orange peel
  1/2 cup firm butter, cut into pieces
   1 cup finely chopped walnuts, *divided*
   1 tablespoon orange juice
GLAZE:
  1/2 cup confectioners' sugar
  1/2 teaspoon grated orange peel
   2 tablespoons orange juice

In a mixing bowl, stir together flour, sugar, salt and peel. Cut in butter until mixture is very crumbly. Mix in 3/4 cup nuts and juice. Press mixture into an ungreased 11-in. x 7-in. x 1-1/2-in. baking pan. Bake at 325° for 35 to 40 minutes or until pale golden brown. Cool slightly. Sprinkle with remaining nuts. Combine glaze ingredients and drizzle evenly over nuts. Cut into 1-1/4-in. squares. Let cool completely in pan on a wire rack; remove from pan and store in airtight container. **Yield:** about 4-1/2 dozen.

※ ※ ※

NO-BAKE CHERRY BALLS

Edna Latimer, Oshawa, Ontario
(PICTURED ON PAGE 27)

Friends and family really look forward to this sweet treat. My husband, Don, likes to eat them right from the freezer! The recipe has been passed down through our family for longer than I can remember.

1-1/2 cups confectioners' sugar
  1/2 cup butter *or* margarine, softened
   1 tablespoon milk
   1 teaspoon vanilla extract
1-1/2 cups shredded coconut
  30 to 36 red and green maraschino cherries with stems
Finely crushed graham cracker crumbs

In a mixing bowl, blend together sugar, butter, milk and vanilla until smooth. Stir in coconut. Chill for 1 hour. Meanwhile, drain cherries on paper towels. Shape about 1 tablespoonful of coconut mixture around each cherry, leaving stem and end exposed. Dip bottom 2/3 of cherry ball in graham cracker crumbs. Refrigerate or freeze until serving. **Yield:** about 2-1/2 dozen.

PFEFFERNEUSSE COOKIES

Deb Schaeffer, Olivet, South Dakota

(PICTURED ON PAGE 27)

Our three boys and I like to make these tiny cookies about a month before Christmas. The longer they are stored, the better the flavor—if you can keep them around that long!

>   1 cup shortening
>   1 cup sugar
>   2 eggs, well beaten
>   1 teaspoon ground cinnamon
>   1/4 teaspoon ground allspice
>   1/4 teaspoon ground cloves
>   1/4 teaspoon ground nutmeg
>   4 tablespoons anise seed
>   1/4 cup light corn syrup
>   1/2 cup molasses
>   1/3 cup water
>   1 teaspoon baking soda
> 6-2/3 cups all-purpose flour

In a large mixing bowl, cream shortening and sugar. Add eggs, spices and anise seed. Combine corn syrup, molasses, water and baking soda. Add to creamed mixture. With mixer, add 3 cups flour; knead in remaining flour by hand. (Dough will be very stiff.) On a lightly floured board, mold dough into long ropes about 1/2-in. in diameter. Chill 1 hour. Slice ropes into 1/3-in. pieces. Place on greased baking sheets. Bake at 400° for 6-8 minutes or until brown as hazelnuts. Cookies will harden upon standing. **Yield:** about 400 cookies.

LITTLE GEMS

Mrs. John E. Taylor, Austin, Colorado

My mother clipped this recipe from the old Cappers Weekly many long years ago. It remains a sweet and festive favorite of mine.

> 1/2 cup butter *or* margarine, softened
> 1/4 cup milk
>   2 teaspoons grated orange peel
>   1 cup all-purpose flour
> 1/3 cup confectioners' sugar
> 1/2 teaspoon salt
> 3/4 cup quick-cooking rolled oats
>   1 cup finely chopped walnuts *or* pecans
>   2 containers (8 ounces *each*) red *or* green candied
>   cherries (about 48 cherries)

GLAZE:
> 1-1/2 cups sifted confectioners' sugar
>   1/2 teaspoon vanilla extract
>   1/4 cup milk

In a mixing bowl, beat butter, milk and orange peel until smooth. Sift together flour, sugar and salt; add to butter mixture. Combine oats and nuts; stir into batter. On a lightly floured surface, roll out dough 1/4 in. thick. Cut into 2-in. circles. Place a cherry in center of each circle. Form dough into a ball around the cherry; remove excess dough. Place on ungreased cookie sheets. Bake at 375° for 16-18 minutes. Combine glaze ingredients. Roll cookies in glaze while warm. Place on racks to cool. **Yield:** about 4 dozen.

CHOCOLATE-ORANGE CRUNCHIES

Karen Ann Bland, Gove, Kansas

(PICTURED ON PAGE 27)

Each Christmas, this recipe gets our family's "hats-off" award for its delicious chocolate and orange combination. I always double the recipe.

>   1 cup shortening
>   2/3 cup packed brown sugar
>   1 egg
>   2 tablespoons orange juice
>   2 cups all-purpose flour
>   1/2 teaspoon salt
>   1/4 teaspoon baking soda
>   1 package (6 ounces) semisweet chocolate chips
>   1/2 cup chopped walnuts *or* pecans
>   2 tablespoons grated orange peel

Sugar

In a mixing bowl, cream shortening and brown sugar. Add egg and orange juice; beat well. Stir together flour, salt and baking soda. Add to creamed mixture and mix well. Stir in chocolate chips, nuts and orange peel. Drop by teaspoonfuls onto an ungreased cookie sheet. Let stand a few minutes; then flatten with a glass dipped in sugar. Bake at 375° for 12-15 minutes or until lightly browned. **Yield:** about 4 dozen.

GINGERBREAD COOKIES

Sarah Dinnen Zimmer, Wauwatosa, Wisconsin

(PICTURED ON PAGE 27)

Shortly after getting married, my mother-in-law gave me this recipe along with "orders" to make it for my husband at Christmas. It's still a family favorite after 32 years!

> 2/3 cup shortening
>   1 cup sugar
>   1 egg
> 1/4 cup light molasses
>   2 cups all-purpose flour
>   1 teaspoon salt
>   1 teaspoon baking soda
>   1 teaspoon ground cinnamon
> 1/2 teaspoon ground ginger
> 1/2 teaspoon ground cloves

In a mixing bowl, cream the shortening, sugar, egg and molasses. Sift together the dry ingredients; beat into the creamed mixture. Add additional flour if necessary. On a lightly floured pastry cloth, roll dough to 1/2-in. thickness. Cut with a decorative 2-1/2-in. cookie cutter dipped in flour. Place on greased cookie sheets. Bake at 375° for 8-10 minutes or until edges are lightly browned. Cool on wire racks. **Yield:** about 3-1/2 dozen.

NUTTY NEWS. Toasting nuts brings out their flavor and aroma. Spread whole or chopped nuts on a cookie sheet in a single layer and bake at 350° until lightly browned, about 5 minutes. Watch carefully.

SWEDISH COOKIES

Jan Yost, Burbank, Ohio
(PICTURED ON PAGE 27)

My grandmother always kept a batch of these cookies in a tin in the freezer. They're delightful.

1-1/2 cups butter *or* margarine, softened
2 cups sugar
2/3 cup unsweetened cocoa
2 tablespoons cold coffee
1 teaspoon vanilla extract
3 cups quick-cooking rolled oats
1 cup finely chopped nuts
Additional sugar

In a mixing bowl, cream together butter and sugar. Add cocoa, coffee and vanilla; mix well. Stir in oats and nuts. Chill. Shape dough into 1-in. balls. Roll in sugar. Store in the refrigerator (may be frozen). **Yield:** about 7 dozen.

LEMON COOKIES

Mrs. Donald McCarron, Chester, Nova Scotia

Winters are long here in Canada, so I like to bake lots of recipes that keep the house warm and smelling good during the holidays. I got this recipe from my mom and it's one of our favorites.

1/2 cup butter *or* margarine
1 cup sugar
1 egg
2 tablespoons lemon juice
1/4 teaspoon lemon extract
1-3/4 cups all-purpose flour
1/2 teaspoon salt
1/2 teaspoon baking soda
1 teaspoon ground ginger
Yellow food coloring, optional
Yellow decorative sugar

In a mixing bowl, cream butter and sugar. Add egg, juice and extract; mix well. Combine dry ingredients; stir into butter mixture. Add a few drops of food coloring if desired. Divide dough into two portions. Shape each onto waxed paper to form a roll 7-in. x 1-1/2-in. Wrap and freeze at least 1 hour. Slice into 1/4-in. cookies. Sprinkle with colored sugar. Bake at 325° for 10-12 minutes. Cool on cookie sheet 1 minute before removing to a cooling rack. **Yield:** about 5 dozen.

CREAM CHEESE DAINTIES

Lynne Stewart, Julian, Pennsylvania

These are a favorite of mine because they're easy to make but look "fussy", which is perfect for the holidays. We have two sons, so the cookies never last long!

1 cup butter *or* margarine, room temperature
1 package (8 ounces) cream cheese, room temperature
2-1/2 cups all-purpose flour

1/2 cup apricot *or* raspberry preserves
Confectioners' sugar, optional

In a mixing bowl, beat butter and cream cheese until well blended. Mix in flour. Divide dough into 4 sections; cover and refrigerate until easy to handle. On a lightly floured surface, roll one piece of dough at a time into a 10-in. x 7-1/2-in. rectangle. Trim edges if necessary. Cut into 2-1/2-in. squares. Spread 1/2 teaspoon preserves diagonally across each square. Moisten the two opposite corners (those without preserves) with water; fold over filling and press lightly. Place on ungreased cookie sheet. Bake at 350° for 12-15 minutes or until corners are lightly browned. Cool 2-3 minutes on cookie sheet before removing to a cooling rack. Sprinkle lightly with confectioners' sugar if desired. **Yield:** 4 dozen.

CHOCOLATE PEANUT BUTTER TOPPERS

Jane Colle, Sterling, Kansas

Here's a pretty cookie for holiday parties or for filling Christmas boxes. It once won 2nd prize in the "party cookies" category at the Kansas State Fair. We love them.

2 cups all-purpose flour
1 cup butter *or* margarine, softened
1/2 cup sugar
2 teaspoons vanilla extract

ICING:
1/4 cup butter *or* margarine
1/3 cup packed brown sugar
1/3 cup creamy peanut butter

CHOCOLATE TOPPING:
1/2 cup semisweet chocolate pieces
2 tablespoons milk
1/3 cup confectioners' sugar

In a mixing bowl, combine flour, butter, sugar and vanilla. Drop by teaspoonsful on greased cookie sheets. Flatten slightly with a glass dipped in sugar. Bake at 325° for 12-14 minutes. Meanwhile, for icing, combine all ingredients and cream until light and fluffy. Spread over warm cookies. Cool on wire rack. For topping, melt chocolate and milk in a small saucepan over low heat. Remove from the heat and beat in sugar. Mix until smooth. Drizzle cookies with topping in a zigzag pattern. **Yield:** about 4 dozen.

COLD COOKIES. Rolled cookie dough, which is sensitive to heat, should be chilled until ready to be cut into shapes.
❉ When rolling the dough, make cutouts close together. For tender cookies, reroll the dough as few times as possible.
❉ To save time, you can bake and freeze gingerbread and butter cookies a few weeks before Christmas; then simply add icing when cookies are needed.

DANDY CANDY! Clockwise from bottom: Peanut Butter Fudge, Double-Dipped Chocolate Bonbons, Stained-Glass Hard Candy, Chocolate Caramel Apples (p. 32).

STAINED-GLASS HARD CANDY

Robbin Thomas, Grouse Creek, Utah
(PICTURED ON PAGE 31)

This candy is a pretty holiday snack to leave out for guests.

        2 cups sugar
    2/3 cup light corn syrup
        1 cup hot water
        1 teaspoon red *or* green food coloring
    1/4 teaspoon cinnamon *or* peppermint candy
            flavoring

In a heavy saucepan, combine sugar, corn syrup and water. Cook over medium heat until the mixture reaches 300° (hard-crack stage). Remove from the heat; add food color and flavorings. Pour mixture onto an oiled cookie sheet. When thoroughly cooled, break into pieces **Yield:** about 1-1/4 pounds.

* * *

DOUBLE-DIPPED CHOCOLATE BONBONS

Janice Grisenti, Rupert, Idaho
(PICTURED ON PAGE 31)

At Christmas, I like to make bonbons and put them on "goody plates" to give to friends and neighbors—if our four sons don't eat them all first!

        1 can (14 ounces) sweetened condensed milk
        4 cups confectioners' sugar
        1 cup butter (no substitutes), softened
        1 teaspoon maple flavoring
    1-1/2 pounds confectionery coating, melted
    1/2 cup chopped toasted almonds

In a mixing bowl, mix milk and sugar. Add butter and maple flavoring. Chill thoroughly. Divide mixture into four or five pieces; freeze until solid. Removing only one piece at a time, roll into 1-in. balls; place on a cookie sheet and freeze until hard. Working with 1 dozen balls or less at a time, dip each ball into the chocolate; place on waxed paper. After chocolate has firmed, dip the candies a second time into the chocolate. Place on fresh waxed paper. Sprinkle immediately with almonds. Refrigerate. **Yield:** 9 dozen.

* * *

PEANUT BUTTER FUDGE

Jane Richmond, Blountville, Tennessee
(PICTURED ON PAGE 31)

Christmas wouldn't be complete without my mother, Cleo Thompson, and I having fun and sharing the love we put into making this fudge. We usually make 12 batches to share with loved ones. Everyone says it's the creamiest they've ever eaten.

        4 cups sugar
    1/2 cup butter *or* margarine
        1 cup evaporated milk
        1 tablespoon vinegar

        1 tablespoon light corn syrup
    Dash salt
        1 jar (12 ounces) chunky peanut butter
        1 jar (13 ounces) marshmallow creme
    1/2 cup finely chopped dry roasted peanuts
        1 teaspoon vanilla extract

Combine sugar, butter, milk, vinegar, corn syrup and salt in a greased 5-qt. Dutch oven or kettle. Cook over medium heat to 236° (soft-ball stage), stirring constantly. Remove from the heat; stir in peanut butter and marshmallow creme. When almost blended, add peanuts and vanilla. Line a 13-in. x 9-in. x 2-in. baking pan with foil; lightly grease it. Pour in fudge; refrigerate until completely cooled. To cut, lift fudge from pan. Remove foil. With a large knife, cut into 1-1/4-in. squares. Store in an airtight container in the refrigerator. **Yield:** about 8 dozen.

* * *

ROCKY ROAD FUDGE

Kathleen Koziolek, Hartland, Minnesota

I modernized this old-time recipe for the microwave, and now it's a fast favorite.

        1 cup light corn syrup
        1 cup sugar
        1 cup creamy *or* chunky peanut butter
        1 package (12 ounces) semisweet chocolate chips
        1 cup salted dry roasted peanuts
        2 cups miniature marshmallows

In a 3-qt. microwave-safe bowl, combine corn syrup and sugar. Mix well. Microwave on high (100% power) until the mixture boils, about 3 minutes. Remove from microwave. Stir in peanut butter; mix until smooth. Add chips, stirring until melted. Stir in peanuts and marshmallows. Immediately pour into a greased and foil-lined 8-in. x 8-in. baking pan. Refrigerate until mixture is firm. Remove foil from pan and cut into 1-in. squares. **Yield:** about 5 dozen.

* * *

CHOCOLATE CARAMEL APPLES

Victoria Schrear, Lowell, Michigan
(PICTURED ON PAGE 31)

I'm an artist, and these apples are a real showpiece at a party. They also taste very good!

        4 wooden sticks
        4 large apples
        1 package (14 ounces) caramels
        2 tablespoons water
        1 cup chopped pecans
        1 package (6 ounces) milk chocolate chips
        1 package (6 ounces) semisweet chocolate chips

Insert wooden sticks in center of clean, dry apples. In a medium saucepan, melt the caramels and water over low heat. Dip apples into caramel mixture, swirling to cover evenly. Immediately roll in nuts, covering the bottom half of the apple. Place on waxed paper; chill. Meanwhile, melt milk chocolate over low heat. Spoon melted chocolate on caramel apples, letting it drip down the sides. Chill. Melt semisweet chocolate; drizzle over milk chocolate. Chill completely. **Yield:** 4 servings.

* * *

HEAVENLY HASH

Mrs. Marvin Lutz, Stevens Point, Wisconsin

My mother has been making this candy for more than 40 years, so making it for my own family brings back delicious memories.

    1 cup coarsely chopped pecans
  36 large marshmallows
    1 cup butter (no substitutes)
 1/2 pound semisweet *or* milk chocolate
    2 bars (4 ounces *each*) German sweet chocolate

Spread pecans on the bottom of a foil-lined 9-in. x 9-in. baking pan. Place marshmallows in six rows. In a saucepan, melt butter and chocolate. Slowly pour over marshmallows and pecans. Refrigerate until firm. Cut into squares. **Yield:** 3 dozen.

* * *

ALMOND BUTTER CRUNCH CANDY

Alice Endreson, Alta, Iowa
(PICTURED ON COVER)

Our children and grandchildren look forward to eating this candy at our house every Christmas. We're retired farmers and have been married 55 years.

    1 cup butter (no substitutes)
    1 cup sugar
    1 tablespoon light corn syrup
    3 tablespoons water
    1 cup slivered almonds
    1 package (6 ounces) semisweet chocolate chips
 1/3 cup chopped almonds

In a heavy saucepan, combine butter, sugar, corn syrup and water. Cook over medium heat, stirring constantly, until the mixture reaches 300° (hard-crack stage). Remove from the heat; stir in slivered almonds. Quickly pour onto a greased metal cookie sheet, forming a 12-in. square. Sprinkle with chocolate chips, spreading with knife when melted. Top with chopped nuts. Cool. Break into 2-in. pieces. **Yield:** about 1 pound.

* * *

FOOLPROOF FUDGE

Debbie Klejeski, Sturgeon Lake, Minnesota

This fudge is a favorite every Christmas. I always have to make a few batches because it never lasts longs.

    3 packages (6 ounces *each*) milk chocolate chips
    1 can (14 ounces) sweetened condensed milk
1-1/2 teaspoons vanilla extract
 1/2 cup chopped nuts

In a heavy saucepan, melt chips and milk over low heat. Remove from heat; stir in vanilla and nuts. Pour into a foil-lined 8-in. x 8-in. baking pan. Chill until firm. Cut into squares. **Yield:** about 5 dozen.

* * *

NUT GOODY BALLS

Beverly Hockel, Odin, Minnesota

These candies taste very rich, but you can never get too many of them.

    1 pound white chocolate *or* white almond bark
    1 package (6 ounces) milk *or* semisweet chocolate chips
 1/2 cup chunky peanut butter
    1 can (12-1/2 ounces) Spanish peanuts

In a heavy saucepan, melt chocolate and peanut butter. Stir in peanuts. Drop by teaspoonfuls onto waxed paper. **Yield:** 6 dozen.

* * *

QUICK & EASY SALTED NUT ROLL

Ruth Ripley, Ottumwa, Iowa

This recipe originated in my sister-in-law's kitchen. It's a festive treat.

    1 package (10 ounces) peanut butter chips
    1 can (14 ounces) sweetened condensed milk
    1 jar (7 ounces) marshmallow creme
    1 can (16 ounces) salted peanuts, *divided*

In a medium saucepan, melt peanut butter chips over low heat. Stir in the milk and marshmallow creme. Remove from heat. Place 2 cups peanuts in the bottom of an 11-in. x 7-in. pan. Pour the hot peanut butter mixture over the peanuts; sprinkle the remaining peanuts on top. Pat down lightly. Freeze until firm. Cut into 1-in. squares. Return to the freezer. **Yield:** about 7-1/2 dozen.

* * *

CHOCOLATE CARAMELS

Kae Clay, Hampton, Iowa

This is an old family recipe—very easy and foolproof. Some years ago, I added the cocoa and really enjoyed the taste. It's been a great seller at annual Christmas bazaars, sold by the piece, and a great gift item, too!

    1 cup sugar
    1 cup light corn syrup
 1/4 cup unsweetened cocoa
 1/4 teaspoon salt
    1 cup whipping cream
 1/4 cup butter (no substitutes), softened
    1 teaspoon vanilla extract

In a heavy saucepan, combine sugar, corn syrup, cocoa and salt. Cook over medium heat until all sugar is dissolved. Meanwhile, in a small bowl, combine the cream and butter; set aside. Heat sugar mixture to a rapid boil and cook to 245°. Gradually add the cream mixture. Continue cooking until the mixture reaches 242°. Remove from the heat; add vanilla and stir until blended. Pour into a greased 8-in. x 8-in. glass baking pan. Do not scrape saucepan. Allow to cool and firm overnight. Invert pan onto a cutting board. With a long sharp knife, using a sawing motion, cut into 3/4-in. squares. **Yield:** about 8 dozen.

GIFTS FROM YOUR KITCHEN

*For close pals or faraway friends, wrap up a
food gift that's sure to be well-received.*

* * *

HOT CHOCOLATE MIX

Sharon Peterson, Lincoln, Nebraska
(PICTURED AT RIGHT)

*I remember my mom serving this often. It makes a large batch, so it can
be packaged nicely as gifts.*

> 1 container (16 ounces) dry chocolate milk mix
> 1 jar (6 ounces) powdered coffee creamer
> 1 box (8 quarts) nonfat dry milk
> 3/4 cup confectioners' sugar
> Marshmallows *or* vanilla ice cream

In a large bowl, combine chocolate milk mix, coffee creamer,
dry milk and confectioners' sugar. To use: Add 1/4 to 1/3 cup
drink mix to 1 cup hot water. Serve with marshmallows or a
small dip of vanilla ice cream. **Yield:** about 9 quarts dry mix.
For Gift-Giving: Place 1-2 quarts of the dry mix in airtight
containers or holiday tins. Be sure to include the recipe and
serving suggestions.

* * *

SOUPER SOUP MIX

Bertha Jones, Czar, Alberta
(PICTURED AT RIGHT)

*A friend gave me this recipe plus dried beans and peas as a Christmas
gift one year. Now I think of her every time I make this delicious soup.*

> 1 pound *each* black-eyed peas, lima beans, pinto
> beans, navy beans, split green peas, red beans, great
> northern beans, lentils, black beans and pearl barley
> 2 tablespoons salt
> Water
> 1/2 pound meaty ham bone *or* hocks
> 1 medium onion, chopped
> 1 can (28 ounces) tomatoes, undrained
> 2 teaspoons chili powder
> 1/2 teaspoon dried thyme
> Juice of 1 lemon
> Salt and pepper to taste
> Dash hot pepper sauce, optional

Combine beans and barley. Use 2-1/2 cups per batch. Wash
bean mixture thoroughly. Place beans in a large bowl; add salt
and enough water to cover. Soak overnight. Drain and rinse.
Place bean mixture, ham bone and 2 qts. water in an 8-qt. soup
kettle. Bring to boil, stirring occasionally. Reduce heat; simmer,
covered, for 2 to 2-1/2 hours. Add remaining ingredients; simmer 30 minutes longer. **Yield:** 3 quarts per batch (10 batches per
recipe). **For Gift-Giving:** Layer 1/4 cup of the barley and 1/4
cup of each bean variety in a canning jar to achieve a rainbow
effect, or combine all and place 2-1/2 cups in a jar or plastic bag.
Seal or tie tightly. Trim with a ribbon and include the recipe.

* * *

TROPICAL CARAMEL CORN

Imogene Humphrey, Florence, Oregon
(PICTURED AT RIGHT)

*This recipe is a favorite of ours at the holidays and is a nice homemade
goody to share with friends.*

> 4 quarts (16 cups) popped popcorn
> 2 cups whole macadamia nuts
> 1-1/3 cups flaked coconut
> 1 cup packed brown sugar
> 1/2 cup butter *or* margarine
> 1/2 cup light corn syrup
> 1 teaspoon vanilla extract
> 1/2 teaspoon baking soda

In a greased jelly roll pan, combine popcorn, nuts and coconut;
set aside. In a saucepan; combine brown sugar, butter and corn
syrup. Cook and stir over medium heat to boiling. Boil 5 minutes
without stirring. Remove from heat; add vanilla and baking soda,
stirring constantly. Pour over popcorn mixture; stir well. Bake at
250° for 45 minutes, stirring every 15 minutes. Remove from the
oven; place on waxed paper to cool. Break apart; store in airtight
containers or plastic bags. **Yield:** about 4 quarts.

* * *

POMANDER BALLS

Virginia Jung, Janesville, Wisconsin
(PICTURED AT RIGHT)

These wonderful gifts are pretty to give and last all year long!

> 3 thick-skinned oranges
> 3 ounces whole cloves
> 1 tablespoon ground cinnamon
> 1 tablespoon Orrisroot*

Wash and dry fruit. Using a skewer to start holes, insert whole
cloves into skins, covering the entire surface of the orange. Mix
cinnamon and Orrisroot; place 1 heaping teaspoon and one orange into a small bag. Shake bag to coat fruit evenly. Repeat with
remaining oranges and cinnamon mixture. Wrap loosely or place
in a foil-covered basket. Store in a dry place until fruit shrinks
and dries. **Yield:** 3 balls. (*Orrisroot is available at craft stores.)
Note: This recipe not edible.

WRAP IT UP. Colorful tins, gift-
wrapped boxes and baskets lined with
cloth and tied with ribbons make festive
containers for giving seasonal snacks.
Tuck your choice of treats, wrapped
in squares of bright cellophane, inside.

TIMELESS TREATS FROM THE KITCHEN. *Clockwise from lower left: Tropical Caramel Corn (p. 34), Pear Conserve (p. 36), Souper Soup Mix (p. 36), Simmering Citrus Potpourri (p. 36), Hot Chocolate Mix (p. 34), Pomander Ball (p. 34), Best-Ever Chocolate Sauce (p. 36).*

SIMMERING CITRUS POTPOURRI

Norma Westhaver, Cilliwack, British Columbia

(PICTURED ON PAGE 35)

This potpourri makes a great gift. I dry fresh orange peels by placing them on paper towel-lined racks overnight. For a special touch, the dried peel can be cut with tiny decorative cookie or canape cutters.

    1 cup dried orange peel, cut into pieces
    1/2 cup dried grapefruit peel, cut into pieces
    1/2 cup broken cinnamon sticks
    1/2 cup whole allspice
    1/2 cup bay leaves
    1/4 cup whole cloves
    1/4 cup anise seed
    1/4 teaspoon orange *or* lemon potpourri oil

In a medium bowl, combine all the ingredients in order listed. Stir to evenly distribute oil. Store in an airtight jar. To use, combine 1 cup water with 2-3 tablespoons potpourri mixture in a saucepan or potpourri burner. Simmer, adding more water as it evaporates. **Note:** Mixture is *not* edible.

CHERRY/RHUBARB JAM

Ilah Bell Flaaten, Fertile, Minnesota

I love to team my homegrown rhubarb with cherries in this jam recipe. It also makes a nice topping for ice cream or for sponge cake, and is a delicious gift!

    6 cups chopped rhubarb
    4 cups sugar
    1 can (21 ounces) cherry pie filling
    1 package (6 ounces) cherry-flavored gelatin

In a mixing bowl, combine rhubarb and sugar; let stand overnight. In a saucepan, cook rhubarb mixture until tender, about 30 minutes. Stir in pie filling and gelatin. Bring to a boil; cool. Pack in containers and refrigerate or freeze until needed. **Yield:** about 7-1/2 pints.

PEAR CONSERVE

Doris Miller, Valley Center, Kansas

(PICTURED ON PAGE 35)

I have made this conserve for many years. My sons are grown and have families of their own, but they still consider this their favorite jam.

    1 orange
    1 can (8 ounces) crushed pineapple, undrained

    14 pounds pears (16 to 18 medium)
    5 cups sugar
    1 jar (8 ounces) maraschino cherries, drained
      and finely chopped

Coarsely grind orange, including peel. In large kettle, combine orange and undrained pineapple. Peel, core and chop pears; add to kettle. Stir in sugar. Bring to boil. Boil, uncovered, 30 to 45 minutes or until thickened, stirring frequently. Stir in cherries. Spoon hot conserve into hot, sterilized jars, leaving 1/2-in. headspace. Adjust lids. Process in boiling-water bath for 15 minutes. **Yield:** 9 12-ounce jars.

BEST-EVER CHOCOLATE SAUCE

Tamara L. Krumm, Oceanside, California

(PICTURED ON PAGE 35)

I've tried many sauce recipes, but this one that I came up with is the tastiest—and a good gift for chocolate lovers. My mom is a great cook and I guess it rubbed off on me! I love to experiment with recipes.

    1/2 cup unsweetened cocoa
    1 cup sugar
    1/4 teaspoon salt
    1 tablespoon cornstarch
    1/2 cup light corn syrup
    1/2 cup milk
    2 tablespoons butter *or* margarine
    2 teaspoons vanilla extract

In a small saucepan, mix dry ingredients. Add corn syrup and milk; blend thoroughly. Bring to a boil; stir and cook for 5 minutes. Remove from the heat. Add butter and vanilla; blend well. Cool slightly before serving. Refrigerate any leftovers. **Yield:** 1-1/2 cups. **For Gift-Giving:** Place in a decorative canning jar; trim with a bow or ruffled cloth cover.

CHOCOLATE COVERED CHERRIES

Karen Kessler, Belfield, North Dakota

I got this recipe years ago from a friend. Everyone loves these cherries at Christmastime. They're a special treat!

    1 cup butter, softened
    1 can (14 ounces) sweetened condensed milk
    2 pounds confectioners' sugar
2-1/2 teaspoons vanilla extract
    2 jars (10 ounces *each*) maraschino cherries with
      stems, well drained
    1 package (12 ounces) semisweet chocolate chips
    1 bar (7 ounces) milk chocolate
    8 ounces paraffin

In a mixing bowl, beat together butter, milk, sugar and vanilla until smooth. Refrigerate mixture until well chilled. With lightly sugared hands, shape tablespoonfuls of mixture around cherries. Place on a cookie sheet and freeze until firm. Meanwhile, combine remaining ingredients in a double boiler; melt over simmering water, stirring occasionally until smooth. Holding onto the stem, dip each frozen ball into the chocolate; set on waxed paper to dry. Refrigerate. **Yield:** about 4 dozen.

HOME, SWEET HOME

THIS CHRISTMAS, be creative and build yourself and your family a brand-new house...a gingerbread house, that is!

Blanche Comiskey of Franklin, Wisconsin used these simple recipes and patterns to construct the candy-coated cottage shown above.

Looking for a fun, unique idea for a holiday get-together? Bake the gingerbread pieces for a number of houses, then invite some friends to come equipped with a bag of candy and let them decorate a house as they wish. After the pieces dry, invite them back to assemble their houses. They'll leave with a completed gingerbread house for their own families to enjoy!

MATERIALS NEEDED: Gingerbread House and Easy Decorator Frosting recipes (below and on page 38); patterns on pages 38 and 39; tracing paper; cardboard; assorted candy for decorating, such as nonpareils, colored jimmies, gumdrops, peppermint wheels, spearmint leaves, Life Savers, candy canes, Christmas suckers, M&Ms, etc.; one sugar cone; 18-in. x 12-in. x 1-in. piece of styrofoam; pastry bag; decorating tips Nos. 18, 21 and 67; cotton balls; Christmas ribbon.

GINGERBREAD HOUSE

    1/2 cup boiling water
      1 cup shortening
      1 cup firmly packed dark brown
        sugar
      1 cup dark molasses
6-1/2 cups all-purpose flour, *divided*
      2 teaspoons baking soda
      2 teaspoons salt
      1 teaspoon ground ginger
      1 teaspoon ground nutmeg
  1/4 teaspoon ground cloves

In a mixing bowl, pour water over shortening. Add sugar and molasses; mix well. Sift together 6 cups flour with remaining dry ingredients; stir into molasses mixture until blended. Wrap in clear plastic wrap and chill overnight.

Trace patterns on pages 38 and 39 onto tracing paper; transfer to cardboard and cut out.

Divide dough into quarters. Roll one quarter 1/4 inch thick on a greased and floured cookie sheet. Using some of the remaining flour, sprinkle a small amount on dough. Place cardboard patterns on the dough and, using a pizza cutter, cut around each piece. (Note: Reverse chimney side to get two "right" sides.) Use a sharp knife to cut around the outline of windows and door. *Do not remove.* Cut only outline of back wall.

Repeat with remaining dough combined with scraps. Continue procedure until all pieces are cut out. Make little gingerbread people, trees or other cutouts with leftover dough.

Bake gingerbread at 375° for 8-12 minutes or until firm to the touch. Be careful that the edges don't get too brown. Remove from the oven and immediately trim with pizza cutter to straighten all seam edges. This is done on each side piece, the center seam of the roof, and the chimney pieces. Leave the other sides of the roof and the shutters as they are baked. Carefully cut out the windows and door along the outline. Discard window pieces but keep the door. Carefully remove pieces from cookie sheets and cool completely on wire racks.

EASY DECORATOR FROSTING

> 6   egg whites
> 1   teaspoon cream of tartar
> 2   pounds confectioners' sugar

In a large bowl, beat egg whites with cream of tartar until soft peaks form. Gradually beat in sugar until frosting is smooth and stiff enough to hold firm peaks. Keep frosting covered with a damp cloth while assembling gingerbread house.

TO DECORATE AND ASSEMBLE HOUSE:
Build house on styrofoam piece. Decorate shutters, door and chimney pieces as desired, using frosting and candies. Let dry. Attach the shutters to the house and allow to dry overnight.

Fill pastry bag with frosting. Using No. 21 decorating tip, pipe a strip of frosting to outline the dimensions of the house. Generously pipe frosting along the back edge of side wall. Press to adjacent end piece and place on the outline established on the styrofoam. Use more frosting on the inside of the seam to reinforce if necessary. Make sure the corner is sealed with frosting. Hold a few minutes to set. Pipe frosting on exposed end of end piece; attach remaining side wall. Pipe frosting along edge of both side walls; attach the front piece and press into place. Pipe frosting along the inside seams to reinforce.

Generously pipe frosting around top edge of house. Set one roof piece in place. Pipe frosting along center seam; set second roof piece in place. Hold until set. Pipe more frosting down center of roof to reinforce. Using No. 18 (star) decorating tip, pipe outline of chimney on roof. Frost each side of chimney and attach to roof. Pull a strip from a cotton ball and attach to inside of chimney to simulate smoke. Decorate roof as desired. If attaching small pieces of candy, work strips a little bit at a time. Decorator frosting dries quickly.

Pipe a "path" from the front door to the edge of the styrofoam. Set the door in place. Trim the door and decorate the path. Reinforce the bottom seams of the house and do the "landscaping".

Using No. 21 (star) tip, pipe an outline around the perimeter of the styrofoam and make a fence out of candy canes, suckers, small gingerbread people, etc.

Place a Christmas tree in the corner of the front yard. To make tree, tint some of the frosting with green food coloring, invert the sugar cone and use the No. 67 (leaf) tip to decorate, starting from the wide point of the cone and working to the top using short strokes around and around. Stop at 1-in. intervals to trim with small candies. Trim the edge of the styrofoam with Christmas ribbon.❊

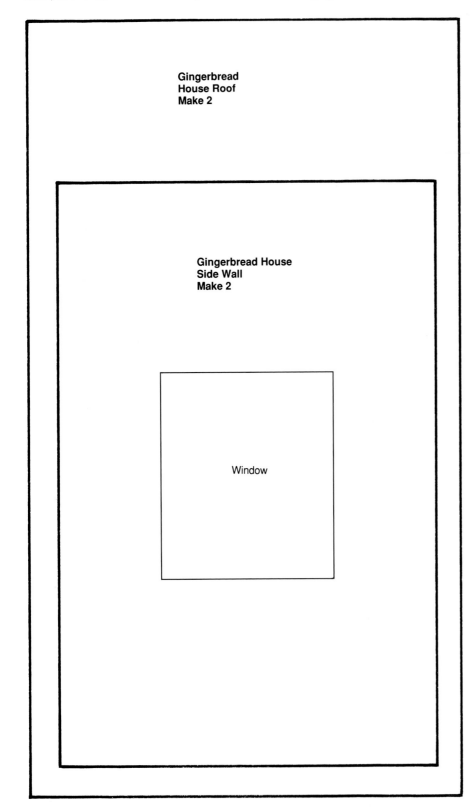

Gingerbread
House Roof
Make 2

Gingerbread House
Side Wall
Make 2

Window

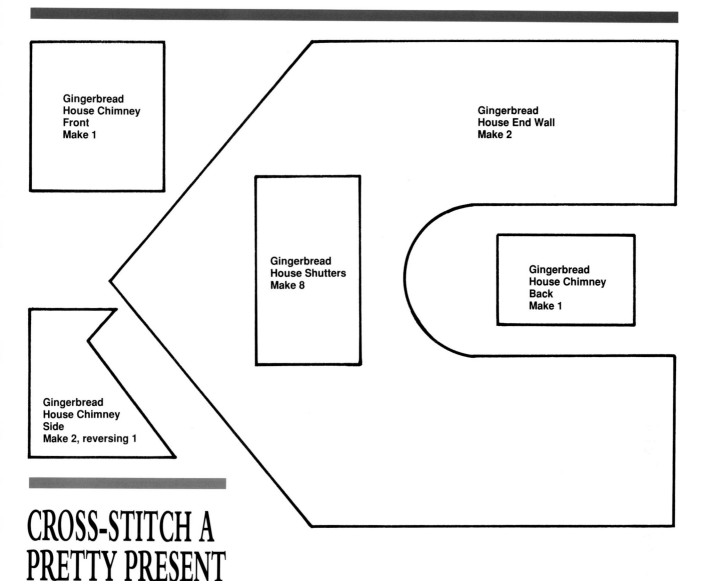

Gingerbread
House Chimney
Front
Make 1

Gingerbread
House End Wall
Make 2

Gingerbread
House Shutters
Make 8

Gingerbread
House Chimney
Back
Make 1

Gingerbread
House Chimney
Side
Make 2, reversing 1

CROSS-STITCH A PRETTY PRESENT

FOR A sweet gift, close up a jar of peppermints with a handmade cross-stitch cover!

CROSS-STITCHED PEPPERMINT JAR

Materials needed: Chart on this page; 6-inch square of 14-count red Aida cloth; DMC six-strand embroidery floss in colors listed on color key; size 24 tapestry needle;

one wide-mouth canning jar with 3-inch lid; 1/3 yard of white beaded eyelet; 2/3 yard of 1/4-inch red satin ribbon; one red ribbon rosebud; one 16-ounce bag of starlight mints (enough for three jars, if desired); hot glue gun; craft glue.

Stitch count: Design area is 36 x 33 stitches to fit the 3-inch jar lid.

Directions: Fold cloth in half, fold in half again to determine center; mark this point. To find center of chart, draw lines across chart, connecting arrows. Begin stitching at this point so design will be centered.

Separate six-strand floss and use two strands for all cross-stitches. Each square on chart equals one stitch over one thread group.

Use two strands of white to back-stitch lettering, to outline candy and to work long stitches to form candy wrapper.

When stitching is completed, wash stitched piece in warm water with a mild soap, only if necessary. Rinse thoroughly. Roll wet piece in terry towel; do not wring. Lay damp piece face down on terry towel and iron dry.

Make a narrow bead of craft glue on the raised part of the inner jar lid. Center stitched piece on top of lid and press edges down, making sure to keep piece flat. Allow to dry. Trim close to edge of jar lid.

Thread ribbon through eyelet beading, saving excess for bow. Use hot glue to glue eyelet to jar ring, folding over 1/2 inch to overlap at end for neat finish at back of jar.

Tie bow and glue to center front of jar ring. Trim ends. Glue ribbon rosebud to center of bow.✳

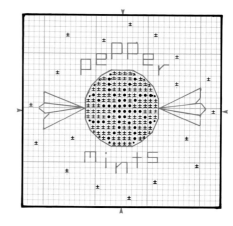

CROSS-STITCHED PEPPERMINT JAR COLOR KEY
⊞ White
◉ Cherry Red   **DMC** 321

HOLIDAY HITS. Pumpkin Cake Roll, Black Forest Torte, Cranberry Apple Pie (recipes on page 41).

SWEETS OF THE SEASON

Make your holiday gathering one to remember with these irresistible desserts.

✳ ✳ ✳

CRANBERRY APPLE PIE

Charlotte Feaser, Boiling Springs, Pennsylvania
(PICTURED AT LEFT)

This pretty pie is the "cranberry apple" of my eye. It's a good country dessert to serve at Christmastime.

```
4 cups thinly sliced peeled baking apples
1 cup fresh or frozen cranberries
1 cup sugar
2 tablespoons cornstarch
1 teaspoon lemon juice
1 teaspoon ground cinnamon
Pastry for double-crust pie (9 inches)
1 tablespoon butter or margarine
```

In a mixing bowl, combine apples, cranberries, sugar, cornstarch, lemon juice and cinnamon. Line a 9-in. pie pan with half the pastry. Spoon filling into crust; dot with butter. Top with a lattice crust. Bake at 400° for 40-50 minutes or until bubbly and golden brown. **Yield:** 8 servings.

✳ ✳ ✳

PUMPKIN CAKE ROLL

Holly Jean VeDepo, West Liberty, Iowa
(PICTURED AT LEFT)

This roll is so good and gets many compliments at family gatherings.

```
3 eggs
1 cup sugar
2/3 cup solid-pack pumpkin
1 teaspoon lemon juice
3/4 cup all-purpose flour
1 teaspoon baking powder
2 teaspoons ground cinnamon
1 teaspoon ground ginger
1/2 teaspoon ground nutmeg
1/2 teaspoon salt
1 cup finely chopped pecans
Confectioners' sugar
FILLING:
1 package (8 ounces) cream cheese, softened
1-1/4 cups confectioners' sugar
5 tablespoons butter or margarine
3/4 teaspoon vanilla extract
```

In a mixing bowl, beat eggs at high speed for 5 minutes or until pale yellow. Gradually beat in sugar. Mix until dissolved. Stir in pumpkin and lemon juice. Stir together dry ingredients and spices; fold into pumpkin mixture. Line a 15-in. x 10-in. x 1-in. jelly roll pan with greased and floured waxed paper. Pour batter into pan. Sprinkle top with pecans; bake at 375° for 15 minutes.

Turn out onto a linen towel dusted with confectioners' sugar. Peel off paper and roll cake up in towel. Let cool. Meanwhile, in a small mixing bowl, beat filling ingredients until smooth. Unroll cake, spread filling to within 1 in. of edges. Roll up again. Refrigerate several hours before serving. Cut into 1-in. slices. **Yield:** 10 servings.

✳ ✳ ✳

BLACK FOREST TORTE

Mrs. Herman Coning, North Manchester, Indiana
(PICTURED AT LEFT)

I ran across this recipe several years ago and love to make it on special occasions like Christmas. Our grown son recently asked for the recipe and went home and made it. He even brought us a slice!

```
CAKE:
1-3/4 cups all-purpose flour
1-3/4 cups sugar
1-1/4 teaspoons baking soda
1 teaspoon salt
1/4 teaspoon baking powder
2/3 cup soft-serve margarine
4 squares (1 ounce each) unsweetened chocolate,
    melted and cooled
1-1/4 cups water
1 teaspoon vanilla extract
3 eggs
CHOCOLATE FILLING:
2 bars (4 ounces each) German sweet cooking
    chocolate, divided
3/4 cup soft-serve margarine
1/2 cup chopped toasted almonds
CREAM FILLING:
2 cups whipping cream
1 tablespoon sugar
1 teaspoon vanilla extract
```

In a mixing bowl, combine all cake ingredients except eggs. Mix at low speed to blend, then beat 2 minutes at medium speed, scraping bowl often. Add eggs; beat 2 more minutes. Pour 1/4 of batter (about 1 cup) into each of four greased and floured 9-in. round cake pans (layers will be thin). Bake at 350° for 15-18 minutes or until cakes test done. Cool slightly and remove from pans. Meanwhile, for chocolate filling, melt 1-1/2 bars of chocolate. Cool. Combine with margarine; stir in almonds. Set aside. For cream filling, combine all ingredients in a small mixing bowl; whip until stiff peaks form. Spread 1/2 of the chocolate filling on one cake layer; spread 1/2 of the cream filling on second layer. Repeat layers, ending with cream filling on top. Do not frost sides. Make chocolate curls with remaining half bar of chocolate to garnish top of torte. Refrigerate until serving time. **Yield:** 16 servings.

Her Holiday House Is
PRETTY IN PINK

Christmas is Heidi Hoffman's favorite time of year—for that special season, she transforms her country home into a fantasyland! Heidi—of Mequon, Wisconsin—enjoys all aspects of country decorating. So during the holidays, with help from her husband, Val, she serves up a feast for the eyes.

And a somewhat surprising one at that, too. Instead of relying on the traditional teaming of red and green, she selects soft pastel accents. They perfectly complement the pinks, mauves and blues in her decor.

The Hoffmans' dining room is dressed its country best all year. A pretty, pastel double wedding ring quilt is the family's everyday tablecloth, and balloon shades and lace lend an elegant look to windows. But Heidi makes it even more inviting this time of year.

She drapes her chandelier in glad greenery. Then she creates a seasonal centerpiece by wreathing a Christmas punch bowl with fragrant pine boughs, sprigs of baby's breath, garlands of beads, clusters of grapes and orange wedges.

Heidi adds timely touches to her living room as well. An antique sleigh (once called on to train farm ponies) serves as a holiday coffee table in front of her country blue couch.

Garlands of green and blue spruce, pink silk poinsettias and strands of beads festoon the Hoffmans' fireplace mantel. And as a finishing touch to this country woman's eye-filling fantasy, miniature lights add a soft glow...while they also give a warm holiday glow to all who come to call.

PASTEL "PALATE"! Festive greenery and quilted tablecloth are a feast for the eyes as Heidi Hoffman pours from her best silver server.

BEST-DRESSED HOUSE. *Tree graced with grapevine garlands complements the country feel in pastel-accented room (left) while teddy bears, dolls and Father Christmas keep company (top left) in Heidi's country collection. Top right, blooming bannister bridges dining, living rooms, while spruced-up fireplace mantel (above) accents the colors in Spanish tiles.*

We Still Keep the
HOME FIRES BURNING

BY BRENDA MORELLI, MOORHEAD, MINNESOTA

For me, one of the wonderful things about winter is curling up in front of the fire. Its friendly snapping and crackling are such good company on a cold night after the children have all been tucked into bed and my farmer husband has nodded off on the couch!

Cozy in my overstuffed chair, wrapped in an old afghan my mother made, I stare through the glowing flames at the red-hot embers. As I do, the satisfying aroma of the wood smoke wafting through the room reminds me of other fires…

I remember one winter when I was just a little girl. An ice storm turned every tree and shrub into a shimmering sculpture. It also snapped the power lines beneath a heavy burden of ice!

We were without electricity for 2 days, and the fireplace provided our only heat. What an adventure! We popped popcorn in an old-fashioned shaker and roasted hot dogs and marshmallows on long, forked sticks.

Huddled around the cozy hearth, we listened to our grandparents' yarns of bygone days. At night, we slept snuggled beneath mounds of quilts right in front of the fireplace—a family pajama party. I was almost disappointed when the electricity was finally restored!

Fellowship around the fireplace is a magical part of country life, especially during the holidays. How well I remember the evenings when my family would gather in front of a blazing fire to sing choruses of carols.

Our homemade stockings hung gaily from the fireplace, and always on the mantel was set a hand-carved Nativity that kept our minds on the true meaning and spirit of Christmas.

This holiday season, I'll lead my own children in joyful choruses of Christmas carols around our fireplace, then help them hang their stockings. In the flickering firelight, I'll marvel once more at the enchanted look on their faces. They'll remind me again that one of the best things about country living is keeping the home fires burning—in our hearths and in our hearts!

Meeting on the Homestead.
Dec 25th 10.

YULETIDE TREASURES

A nostalgic "page from the past" featuring cherished family photos and stories at Christmastime.

Humble Beginnings. *"My newlywed parents (third and fourth from left in photo at left) shared a Black Hills Christmas with fellow homesteaders outside their tar paper shack in 1910," Palma Isakson, Colton, South Dakota, recounts.*

Better Not Cry! *It's hard to tell if Carole Ford, Hickory Hills, Illinois (left), was shy of camera or of Santa at 10 months old! "Money for photos like this was scarce during the Depression, so I treasure this shot," she remarks.*

Gift from the Past. *Pensive lad pondering an ornate evergreen in 1918 photo below is Karen Trentzsch's dad, Randall Noper. "My children still use that old oak rocker," Karen writes from Canon City, Colorado.*

1939

A MERRY CHRISTMAS

Weighed Down with "Wishes". *"My uncle was about ready to start on his postal route in rural Michigan when this photograph (above) was taken," notes Mary Hiter of Benton, Kentucky. "I don't know the exact date, but Christmas could not have been far off—his car is full of Montgomery Ward mail-order catalogs!"*

Romantic Drift. *"This is the way that my parents spent their first Christmas together," reports Betty Gibbs, Hanceville, Alabama. "Dad had to shovel for a block to free them from Wisconsin blizzard of 1925."*

I'll Never Forget Gram's
KITCHEN TOMATOES

BY DOREEN G. HOWARD OF FREEPORT, TEXAS

It was just before the first hard freeze of 1944 that Gram went to her garden—and began my introduction to the growing power of pixie fairies! With World War II requiring a special effort of everyone, my mother worked 14-hour days in a defense plant in Fort Worth. My father was in the Army somewhere in Europe.

So I—a lonely 4-year-old—lived with Gram on the family farm, near the Red River just north of Paris, Texas.

My world was filled with older people attuned to the rhythm of nature. There was little to entertain a small child, though. Gram must have noticed that—and known what to do about it.

In her garden that fall day, she stripped all the tomato vines of their green fruit. Each pale globe was wrapped in newspaper and stored in boxes in the pantry to ripen.

"There are enough tomatoes to take us through January," Gram announced. "But it will be June until I see another fresh one—unless I plant kitchen tomatoes."

Kitchen tomatoes? My young imagination envisioned vines snaking around the tin sink, over the water pump and into the wood cookstove!

Gram, of course, had something else in mind. She pushed tiny seeds into four pots full of garden dirt and placed them on the windowsill. Then she tied back the curtains so the plants would receive plenty of light.

By Thanksgiving, the kitchen tomatoes were a foot high and producing their first flowers. It was my daily job to gently tap those flowers—"just like the bees do outside," Gram explained.

Before long, however, Christmas was upon us. My mother arrived for a joyous reunion, and an enormous par-cel—containing a porcelain doll with long, golden ringlets—was delivered from France. The tomatoes faded from my mind…until a snowfall brought me to the window.

"Gram," I gushed, "it's magic! The vines are so big. Pixies must have sprinkled stardust on them!"

My grandmother chuckled. "No, sweetie. They've all been growing steady. I told you if they had sunshine they would."

Weeks more went by. I spent my afternoons basking in the brightness of the window and warming my hands with hot cocoa as I admired the pale green fruit putting on size. And when seed catalogs started arriving, I also began work on my own "garden" project.

After Gram had placed her seed orders, I was allowed to take my scissors to the florid drawings in those wintertime wish books. Then—with a paste Gram concocted from flour and water—I carefully glued my paper garden all over an old cigar box. What a wonderful surprise it would make for Mama, I thought!

Gram's tomatoes soon stretched my patience, though. They were turning red ever so S-L-O-W-L-Y. I desperately wanted to enjoy a thick slice of one on a piece of homemade honey wheat bread slathered with mayonnaise. Couldn't those pixies speed up the magical process?

Finally, the day came when Gram picked the first one. The occasion coincided happily with another visit by my mother.

"Oh, Mama!" she exclaimed, wiping away a tear, when Gram showed her the wintertime harvest. "Kitchen tomatoes. And the *most* beautiful jewelry box in the world from my daughter," she added, patting my hand-made present. "It almost makes me forget about the war."

We enjoyed fresh kitchen tomatoes for weeks. And it was shortly before Gram's outdoor tomatoes ripened in June that—amid great jubilation—World War II ended in Europe. My mother came back to the farm to wait with me for my father's return from France; he was home 3 months later, and we moved to Dallas.

Every Christmas afterward, for as long as she lived, we spent at my grandmother's farm. But there were never kitchen tomatoes in the window again. Mama said it was because Gram didn't have a little girl anymore to shake the flowers.

Today the grandmother is *me*. My sunny country kitchen window is filled with tomatoes each winter, and I have two small granddaughters —with their own visions of pixies—who love to shake the flowers.

There's one difference, however. I make sure to plant fast-growing varieties. You see, I recall exactly how impatient a little girl can be!

HOLIDAY CHEER

Christmas wrappings on the floor,
A choir of carolers at the door,
A tall and twinkling Christmas tree
Bedecked with lights for all to see,

Sparkling ornaments so jolly,
Fragrant pine and shiny holly,
Bells that ring out Christmas cheer
To guide us through the coming year.

By Ericka Northrop
Tucson, Arizona

MAKING MERRY

What makes a "merry" Christmas
From dawn till close of day?
Is it the tree that proudly stands
With lights and trimmings gay,
And all the magic packages
Beneath in foil so bright?
Is it the sparkling snowflakes
That clothe the world in white?

Is it the homemade welcome wreath
That hangs upon the door,
Or perhaps the rich aromas
That from the kitchen pour?
The joy of having loved ones
Together for a while,
The handclasp of true friendship,
Or a neighbor's ready smile?

Stars that shine in children's eyes
When Santa Claus they see,
The story of the Christ Child
And of the wise men three?
Ah yes, much Christmas happiness
Each one of these imparts—
Entwined and held so tenderly
By love within our hearts.

By Beulah Sutton Waite
Sullivan, Illinois

A COUNTRY CHRISTMAS

Oh, it's a country Christmas
That I am dreaming of,
With candles in the windows
And a home that's filled with love.

With children singing carols
As they trim the Christmas tree;
And Mother in the kitchen
Baking treats for you and me.

A church upon the hillside,
And moonlight on the snow,
Oh, it's a country Christmas
That casts a special glow.

By Loise Pinkerton Fritz
Lehighton, Pennsylvania

THE FIRST NOËL

Traditional English Melody

1. The first No-ël the an-gel did say Was to
2. They look-ed up and saw a star Shin-ing
3. This star drew nigh to the north-west, O'er
4. Then en-ter'd in those wise-men three, Full

cer-tain poor shep-herds in fields as they lay; In fields where they lay
in the East, be-yond them far, And to the earth it
Beth-le-hem it took its rest, And there it did both
rev-'rent-ly up-on their knee, And of-fer'd there, in

keep-ing their sheep, On a cold win-ter's night that was so deep.
gave great light, And so it con-tin-ued both day and night.
stop and stay Right o-ver the place where Je-sus lay.
His pres-ence, Their gold and myrrh and frank-in-cense.

No-ël, No-ël, No-ël, No-ël, Born is the King of Is-ra-el.

GOOD KING WENCESLAS

Words by John Mason Neale
Music Traditional

ANGELS WE HAVE HEARD ON HIGH

Traditional French carol

Joyously

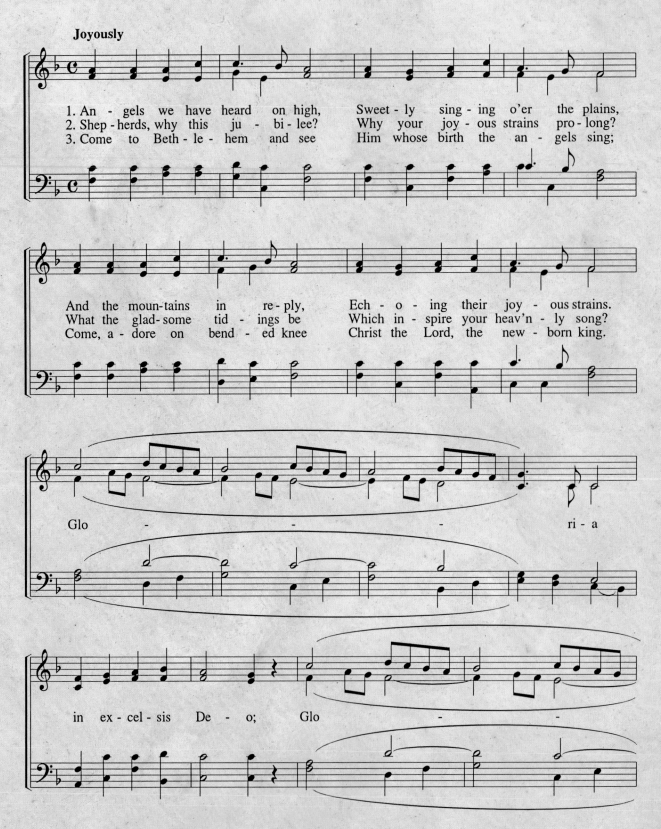

1. An - gels we have heard on high, Sweet - ly sing - ing o'er the plains,
2. Shep - herds, why this ju - bi - lee? Why your joy - ous strains pro - long?
3. Come to Beth - le - hem and see Him whose birth the an - gels sing;

And the moun - tains in re - ply, Ech - o - ing their joy - ous strains.
What the glad - some tid - ings be Which in - spire your heav'n - ly song?
Come, a - dore on bend - ed knee Christ the Lord, the new - born king.

Glo - - - ri - a

in ex - cel - sis De - o; Glo - -

ri - a in ex - cel - sis De - o.

AWAY IN A MANGER

Tenderly

1. A - way in a man - ger, no crib for a bed, The lit - tle Lord
2. The cat - tle are low - ing, the ba - by a - wakes, But lit - tle Lord
3. Be near me, Lord Je - sus; I ask Thee to stay Close by me for -

Je - sus laid down His sweet head. The stars in the bright sky looked
Je - sus, no cry - ing He makes. I love Thee, Lord Je - sus! Look
ev - er and love me, I pray. Bless all the dear chil - dren in

down where He lay, The lit - tle Lord Je - sus a - sleep on the hay.
down from the sky, And stay by my cra - dle till morn - ing is nigh.
Thy ten - der care, And take us to heav - en to live with Thee there.

Text: author unknown c. 1883, sts. 1-2; John T. McFarland, 1851-1913, st. 3, alt.
Tune: William J. Kirkpatrick, 1838-1921

CRADLE SONG

WHAT CHILD IS THIS?

Words by William Chatterton Dix
Traditional English Tune, "Greensleeves"

1. What Child is this, Who, laid to rest, On Mary's lap is sleep - ing? Whom
2. Why lies He in such mean es - tate, Where ox and ass are feed - ing? Good
3. So bring Him in - cense, gold and myrrh, Come peas - ant, king, to own Him, The

an - gels greet with an - thems sweet, While shep - herds watch are keep - ing?
Chris - tian, fear: for sin - ners here The si - lent Word is plead - ing:
King of kings sal - va - tion brings, Let lov - ing hearts en - throne Him.

This, this is Christ the King, Whom shep - herds guard and an - gels sing:
Nails, spear, shall pierce Him through, The Cross be borne, for me, for you:
Raise, raise the song on high, The Vir - gin sings her lul - la - by:

Haste, haste to bring Him laud, The Babe, the Son of Ma - ry!
Hail, hail the Word made flesh, The Babe, the Son of Ma - ry!
Joy, joy for Christ is born, The Babe, the Son of Ma - ry!

OH CHRISTMAS TREE
OH TANNENBAUM

Traditional German

(First two lines of each stanza to be repeated.)

2. Oh Christmas Tree, Oh Christmas Tree,
   You are the tree most loved!
   How often you give us delight
   In brightly shining Christmas light!
   Oh Christmas Tree, Oh Christmas Tree,
   You are the tree most loved!

3. Oh Christmas Tree, Oh Christmas Tree,
   Your beauty green will teach me
   That hope and love will ever be
   The way to joy and peace for me.
   Oh Christmas Tree, Oh Christmas Tree,
   Your beauty green will teach me.

SIMPLE GIFTS

BY CAROLE NIELSON, SHADY COVE, OREGON

My family was never closer than the year I was 12 years old, when we were facing our first Christmas on our Oklahoma farm. We had moved from Oregon that summer, packing up everything we couldn't sell. My dad longed to try his hand at farming, as his father had, so we bought 190 Sooner acres and 50 head of cattle.

So far, it hadn't been a good move. By Thanksgiving, the cattle market had plummeted and we had very little money. Cows that had cost $150 a head were now selling for $35. Daddy swore he'd eat every one of them before he sold at that price. Mother told me, with tears in her eyes, there wouldn't be any money for Christmas presents.

But I knew better. Hidden in a miniature cedar chest in my closet was the money I'd earned from baby-sitting, picking strawberries, and selling our surplus eggs. My parents needed a new radio, since their old one got mostly static, and I intended to buy them one.

Daddy liked to listen to the news every evening, and Mother enjoyed hearing *The Breakfast Club* while she did the morning dishes, separated the milk and churned the butter. Evenings, our family would gather around the radio to catch the latest episode of *Gunsmoke* or *Dragnet*; *The Grand Ole Opry* and *Louisiana Hayride* were favorites, too.

A quick check of our Sears, Roebuck catalog told me I was a few dollars short of having enough for a new radio, so I made myself available for baby-sitting at every opportunity to save more.

The big day finally arrived a few days before Christmas, when I rode into town with my girlfriend Carolyn Trogdon and her mother. I took every penny I had, but when I found the radio I wanted, I was still $2.52 short.

Mrs. Trogdon offered to lend me the rest and said I could work it off by helping bottle-feed their orphaned calves for two evenings. The deal was made—I had the perfect gift for my parents!

Christmas morning dawned crisp and clear, and I woke to the delicious smells of buttermilk biscuits and sizzling home-cured bacon. As I sat up and rubbed my eyes, I saw a beautiful suede jacket hanging next to my closet. I jumped out of bed, grabbed the jacket and ran into the kitchen, where Mother was cooking and Daddy was setting the table.

"What's this?" I blurted.

"Why, it's your Christmas present," Mother answered matter-of-factly.

"But I thought you didn't have any money to buy presents. Where did you get this? It's beautiful!"

"I made it from the hide of a deer your dad killed and had tanned while we were still in Oregon," Mother said. "Daddy helped me cut it out a few weeks ago, and I sewed on it during the day while you were in school."

"It fits perfectly," I murmured as I slipped it on.

"I thought it would," Mother said with a smile. "I fitted it on your friend Carolyn."

"And she kept it a secret all this time," I laughed.

After I hugged, kissed and thanked my parents, I scurried to my closet and pulled the radio out of its hiding place. They were even more pleased and surprised than I imagined they'd be.

I learned a lesson for life that day—that it doesn't take much money to have a memorable family holiday. It turned out to be a wonderful Christmas!

❊ ❊ ❊

It's the handmade gifts we hold most dear. Whether it's a teddy bear made long ago by Grandmother or a soft knit sweater that's been handed down through the family, homemade Christmas presents can kindle powerful memories.

Now you can make memorable gifts for others, too, by delving into several of the simple craft projects on the following pages.

The best Christmas gifts aren't expensive ones... they're the ones that come from the heart.

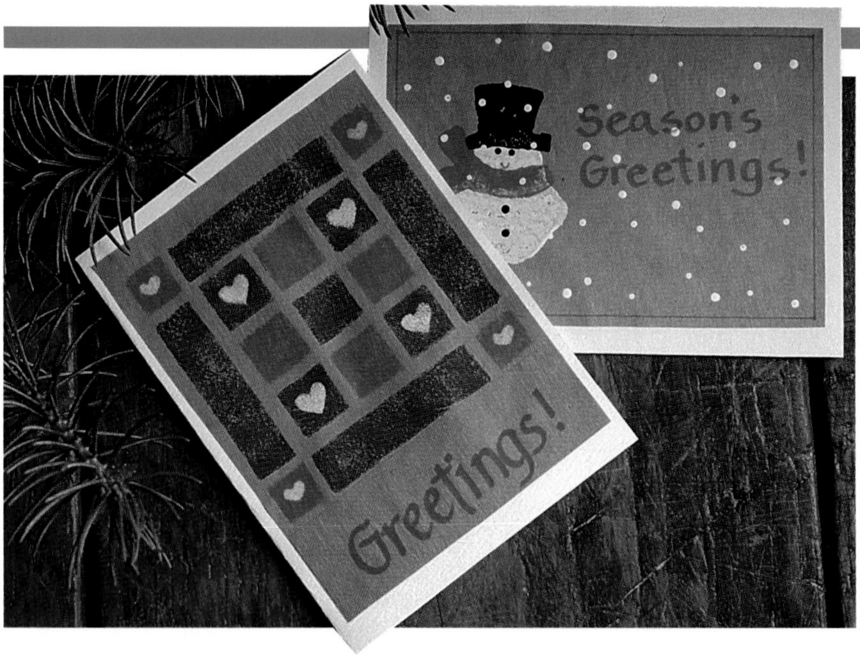

CREATE YOUR OWN CARDS!

SEND A special holiday "hello" to friends and relatives with handmade greeting cards. Making the inexpensive cards can be great family fun. Just use potatoes and brown paper!

POTATO PRINT AND STENCILED CARDS

Materials needed: Patterns; tracing paper; pencil; solid brown wrapping paper; 8- x 11-1/2-inch sheets of stiff white drawing paper; red calligraphy marker with 2.0mm nib; red fine-line permanent-ink marker; glue stick; acrylic craft paints—white, red, green and black; tape; ruler; paper towels; container of water; plastic lid for palette.

FOR POTATO PRINT: Several large raw potatoes; lightweight cardboard; paring knife; flat artist's brush; stylus or small paintbrush.

FOR STENCILED CARD: Small stencil brush; stencil acetate; stencil knife or craft knife with sharp No. 11 blade.

Directions: Tape brown paper to flat surface. Use ruler and pencil to mark 3-3/8- x 5-inch rectangles for potato printed cards and 3-3/4- x 5-inch rectangles for stenciled cards.

Print designs on brown paper as directed in individual instructions, referring to photo for placement. When dry, remove tape and cut out rectangles on marked lines. Cut heavy white paper into 8- x 5-1/2-inch rectangles and fold into 4- x 5-1/2-inch cards. Glue printed designs to front of cards.

POTATO PRINT: Trace snowman's body, scarf and hat patterns. Glue patterns to cardboard and cut out. Wash, dry and cut potatoes in half across width (not length), placing cut sides down on a paper towel to absorb excess moisture.

Making one stamp per shape, place cardboard patterns on cut sides of potatoes and trace around patterns with pencil. Use pointed end of paring knife to outline shapes with 1/4- to 1/2-inch-deep cuts. Slice away excess potato outside traced lines, creating raised shapes. Place stamps cut side down in a shallow pan of water.

Drain stamps, cut side down on paper towel, for about 5 minutes before stamping. Place a small amount of white paint on palette and brush a thin even layer on snowman stamp. Practice stamping design on scrap paper. When satisfied with results, print design on brown paper rectangles, reapplying paint for each new print.

When dry, stamp red scarf and black hat on each snowman. Dip stylus or tip of small paintbrush handle in black paint and dab on snowman for eyes and buttons. Draw mouth in with red fine-line marker.

When dry, use red fine-line marker and ruler to draw a border 1/8 inch in from all edges of rectangle. Use calligraphy marker to print "Season's Greetings". Dip stylus or tip of brush handle in white paint and randomly add dots to resemble falling snow.

STENCILED CARD: With fine-line marker, trace design twice on acetate, leaving ample room between tracings. Place acetate on a thick layer of newspaper to protect work surface. Holding craft or stencil knife like a pencil, begin at top of each shape and slowly pull knife until each shape A is cut from first tracing and each shape B is cut from second tracing. Repair cutting mistakes by applying tape to both sides of acetate and recutting. Cut two heart stencils in same way.

Place a small amount of red paint on palette. Position stencil A on a brown paper rectangle. Dip stencil brush in paint and remove excess by wiping brush on a folded paper towel. (Too much paint can seep under stencil edges, ruining the design.) Hold brush perpendicular to stencil, and dab brush in an up and down motion over cutout areas of stencil. Stencil all of design A. When finished, clean brush with soap and water and wipe with paper towel so brush is nearly dry. (A wet brush can cause paint to seep under stencil.)

Position stencil B over design, using uncut traced areas as an aid in placement. With green paint, stencil design same as before. When dry, stencil small white hearts in center of each red corner square, and larger white hearts in center of green squares (see photo). Use calligraphy marker to print "Greetings!" below stenciled design.❄

POTATO PRINT PATTERNS

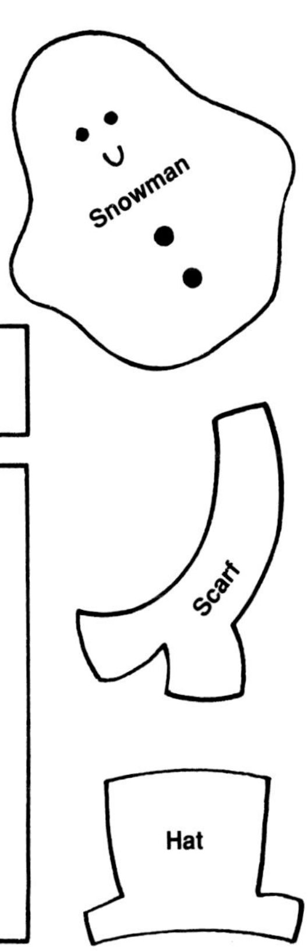

STENCILED CARD PATTERNS

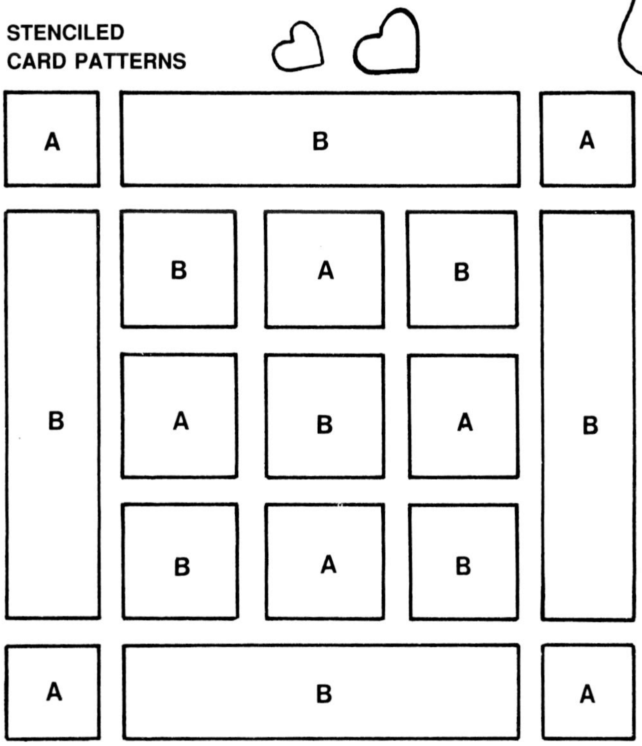

CAPS FOR KIDS

BY BEA KARNES OF SAN JOSE, CALIFORNIA

EVERYONE loves a heartwarming Christmas story. Bonnie Greene's homespun yarn warms the ears, too!

"I'm a knitter and the owner of a yarn shop in San Jose, California," Bonnie begins. "And I found that when I'd finish a knitting project, I always had a little yarn left over. My customers told me they had the same 'excess' problem."

Not one to scrap otherwise usable scraps, Bonnie put on her thinking cap—and came up with a better idea..."Caps for Kids".

"There are so many needy children in the world. I thought to myself, 'Why not make the Christmas season just a little bit nicer for them?'"

So that same year, Bonnie and her band of nimble-fingered knitters created 640 caps from scattered scraps. It was a bright beginning—but just the tip of the hat in comparison to last year's inspiring output of 75,000 caps in all.

Bonnie's kids, knitters—and caps —now cover the nation. "We have 43 states involved in the 'Caps for Kids' program," she beams. "Plus people are participating overseas, as far away as Australia!"

Wherever they work, the volunteer knitters are aided by some compassionate craft concerns. Yarn manufacturers turn over their surplus to shops. The stores then supply free yarn, needles, crochet hooks and patterns to "Caps for Kids" knitters.

Age is no obstacle. In fact, Bonnie points out, "Senior citizens are some of our most enthusiastic helpers. Many of them have some free time, and they enjoy doing something worthwhile with it. I know two women, for example, who've each made and donated over 1,000 hats a year for children!"

That is what makes the "Caps for Kids" program stand out above the rest, Bonnie believes.

"There's a wonderful feeling that comes from doing something for others without expecting anything in return," she says. "At Christmas—or anytime— it's the very *best* gift you can get!"

If you'd like to take part in "Caps for Kids", ask at your local yarn shop. Shops can get involved by sending a self-addressed stamped envelope to "Caps for Kids", 1701 Willow Pass Rd. No. E, Concord CA 94520.

WINTER WARMER

HELP keep a child cozy this Christmas by following these fast instructions to knit a cute cap.

KNITTED CAP

Materials needed: 4 ounces 4-ply worsted-weight yarn (sport-weight yarn can be used with 2 strands) in one or more colors; size 6 straight knitting needles; yarn needle.

Finished size: Instructions are for infant size 1 cap with child under 10 size in ( ).

Gauge: 18 sts and 28 rows equal 4 inches.

KNITTING ABBREVIATIONS

k	knit
k 2 tog	knit 2 stitches together
p	purl
psso	pass slipped stitch over
sl 1	slip one stitch
st	stitch

Directions: Starting at cuff, cast on 78(105) sts.

Row 1: K 2, * p 2, k 2. Repeat from * across row.

Row 2: P 2, * k 2, p 2. Repeat from * across row.

Rep rows 1 and 2 for 12(16) rows. These rows can be made in stripes, working 4 rows each of different colors and the remainder of the cap with main color.

With main color, knit 1 row. Rep 2nd and 1st row until total length is 6(8) inches.

Dec Round: * K 2 tog, k 1. Rep from * across row: 52(70) sts remain.

Continue working knit one row, purl one row for 1-1/2(2) inches.

Rep dec round and work 1(1-1/2) inches more: 35(47) sts remain.

Rep dec round and work 1/2 inch more: 24(32) sts remain.

Break off, leaving a 20-inch length of yarn. Thread this length into needle and slip remaining sts onto it. Draw together tightly and fasten securely on wrong side. Sew a 4(5)-inch back seam starting at top; then reverse seam, stitching from wrong side of cap for turn-up. Attach a pom-pom, tassel or button, if desired.

INFANT EAR FLAPS: Cast on 15 sts.

Row 1: Sl 1, k 14.

Row 2: P 14, k 1.

Row 3-6: Repeat rows 1 and 2.

Odd Rows 7-15: K 2, sl 1, k 1, psso, k to last 4 stitches, k 2 tog, k 2.

Even Rows 8-16: Purl.

Row 17: K 2 tog, k 1, k 2 tog.

Cut yarn, leaving tail. Thread tail through last 3 sts and weave in end. Cut ribbon in half, sew each to end of flap with matching thread. Use 9 strands of yarn to make a 12-inch braid, knotting both ends and trimming threads close. Sew braid to narrow end of ear flap.

Fold up 2-1/2 inches of lower edge of hat. Sew ear flap so inner edge is 5 inches from back seam.

Repeat for other earflap.✻

WHAT, LOST YOUR MITTENS?

IF YOU'RE tired of hunting for lost mittens or need a place to hang wet gloves, here's the solution! Simple clothespins hold several soggy woolens to dry and help keep pairs from getting misplaced. With its antique look and easy design, this mitten rack also makes an excellent gift that's sure to get a workout each winter.

MERRY MITTEN RACK

Materials needed: Pattern; tracing paper; pencil; 12-inch-long x 8-inch-wide piece of 1-inch pine lumber (1-inch pine is actually about 3/4 inch thick); 12-inch-long x 4-inch-wide piece of 1-inch pine lumber; four spring-type clothespins; band or scroll saw; fine sandpaper; tack cloth; drill with 1/4-inch bit; two 1-3/4-inch lengths of 1/4-inch-thick dowel; artist's brushes—No. 6 flat and No. 10/0 liner; 1-inch sponge brush; Folk Art acrylic paints—Southern Pine, Raspberry Wine and Butter Pecan; Folk Art antiquing

—Wood'n Bucket Brown; water-base varnish; medium-brown water-base stain; paper towels; wood glue; two triangle hangers; hammer.

Directions: Trace mitten pattern to tracing paper and cut out. Place pattern on 8-inch-wide lumber and trace two mittens. Cut out with band or scroll saw. Sand edges smooth. Drill 1-inch-deep holes in center of bottom of mittens where indicated on pattern. Drill two 1-inch deep holes in top 12-inch edge of 12-inch piece of lumber, drilling 3-1/4 inches from each outer edge. Remove dust with tack cloth.

Use sponge brush to apply stain to all surfaces of mittens and 12-inch piece, including the edges. Also stain clothespins. Wipe off excess stain with paper towels.

Using sponge brush, paint front and side surfaces of both mittens (making sure to reverse one mitten) with Southern Pine. Let dry. Using flat brush, paint Raspberry Wine stripes for cuffs. When dry, paint Butter Pecan X's on stripes with liner brush. Let dry.

Sand mitten surfaces, sanding more heavily on edges. Clean with tack cloth. Using paper towels, apply antiquing to mittens, rubbing off excess with clean paper towels. Let dry several hours.

Apply two coats of water-base varnish to all surfaces of mittens and 12-inch piece, letting dry between coats. Put wood glue in holes of mittens and 12-inch piece.

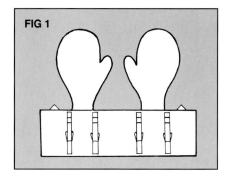

Insert dowels into holes of 12-inch piece and slide mittens over dowels. Let dry on flat surface.

Glue clothespins in place, lining up inner edges of clothespins with outer cuff edges of mittens. Allow to dry. Tack hangers on back of top straight edge, about 1 inch from corners. See Fig. 1. ❋

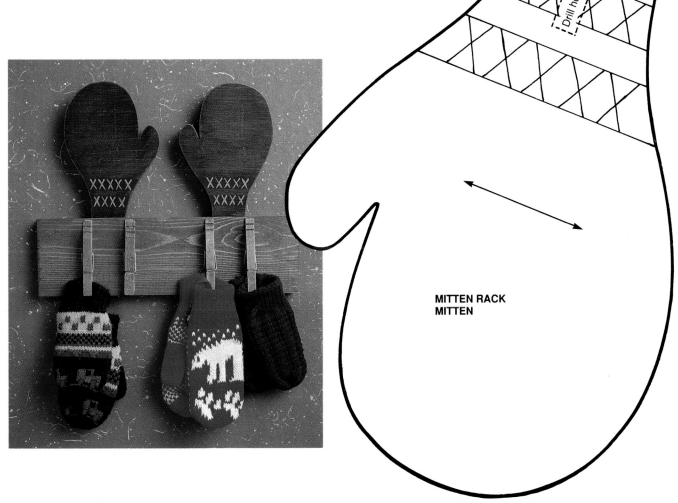

**MITTEN RACK
MITTEN**

Drill hole for dowel

CUDDLE UP FOR CHRISTMAS

INTERESTED IN a way to breathe new life into old wool sweaters? Turn them into a warm and wooly "Wadmal" bear! This cuddly critter—made from 100% wool using a Scandinavian technique called Wadmal—is bound to delight a doll-loving child or crafter for many years to come.

WADMAL BEAR

Materials needed: Pattern; one 9- x 16-inch piece of shrunken 100% wool knit fabric in appropriate color (see Wadmal instructions below); matching heavy-duty thread; 1-1/2- x 18-inch piece of tightly knit colorful wool for scarf; two 9mm animal eyes; four 1/2-inch two-hole buttons; small amount of black sport- or worsted-weight yarn; long soft-sculpture or doll needle; crewel embroidery needle; craft glue or hot glue gun; disappearing-ink fabric marking pen; polyester stuffing; standard sewing supplies.

Note: This bear is not suitable for a child under the age of 3.

Wadmal: To make a 9- x 16-inch piece of shrunken fabric, begin with a much larger piece of 100% wool knit fabric (it can be new or from an old garment such as a sweater). Wash the fabric in hot water and rinse it in cold water. Dry in a very hot dryer so it shrinks and forms a thick, felt-like fabric that will not ravel when cut. Wadmal is the Scandinavian term for this technique, which will only work if the fabric is 100% wool.

To find out whether or not a piece is 100% wool, snip off a tiny piece and carefully set it on fire. The smell should resemble the smell of burning hair and the ash should crumble into nothing. Man-made fibers form a hard ball rather than an ash.

Directions: Fold fabric in half vertically so wrong sides are together. Use disappearing-ink marker to trace around pattern pieces on top half of folded fabric, making certain pattern pieces are placed so arrows match the direction with the most stretch. Do not cut out the fabric.

Arms and legs: Sew two layers together right on tracing lines, leaving openings for turning as marked on pattern. Sew with straight, not zigzag, stitches.

Cut out each piece 1/8 inch from stitching. This is right side of piece. The seam allowance will be on the outside, so cut carefully. Insert stuffing and topstitch openings closed.

Body: Sew around body on tracing lines. Leave open as marked on pattern. Cut out same as for limbs. Cut out head inset. Pin inset in place, matching letters B and F. Sew in place with a 1/8-inch seam allowance. Trim seam if necessary to make it uniform with rest of seam on bear.

Stuff bear's muzzle, then head. Stuff his cheeks so they are full and round. Stuff the neck and body next. Pay attention to the shape and symmetry of your bear as you insert the stuffing. When satisfied, topstitch back opening closed.

Use a soft-sculpture or doll needle and heavy thread to stitch legs to body. Place a two-hole button on outside of each leg and sew back and forth through legs, body and buttons several times. See pattern for position. Determine where you wish to place arms and attach in same way.

Finishing: Use crewel embroidery needle and black yarn to embroider nose with satin stitches and mouth with two straight stitches. Hand-stitch ears in place. See pattern for placement.

Hand-sew a few stitches in bear's head where each eye will be placed. Catch some of the stuffing in each stitch and pull the thread taut so an eye socket is formed. Cut shanks off back of animal eyes and glue eyes to sockets.

Scarf: Make a number of 1-1/2-inch-deep slits on each short end of the 1-1/2- x 18-inch piece of wool to make ends look fringed. See photo. Tie scarf around bear's neck. ✻

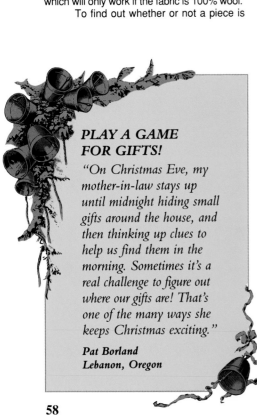

WADMAL BEAR EAR
Cut 2—Wadmal fabric

Most stretch

Most stretch

WADMAL BEAR LEG
Trace 2 on doubled Wadmal fabric

Leave open

Leave open

Ear placement

WADMAL BEAR
HEAD AND BODY
Trace 1 on
doubled Wadmal fabric

O

B

B

Satin stitch

Straight stitch

Leave open

WADMAL BEAR ARM
Trace 2 on doubled Wadmal fabric

WADMAL BEAR
HEAD INSET
Cut 1—Wadmal fabric

Most stretch

Most stretch

Leave open

Most stretch

F

F

Leg placement

WHAT A BRIGHT IDEA!

SHOW LOVED ONES how sweet they are with candle holders made of candy canes. Inexpensive and easy to assemble, these candle confections are "tasteful" gifts for friends as well as quick projects for a Christmas bazaar. Try experimenting with different colored canes, then garnishing with ribbons, beads or silk flowers.

CANDY CANE
CANDLE HOLDERS

Materials Needed: 4-inch piece of 3/4-inch-diameter PVC pipe; 12 candy canes (6-inch-long); 1 candy wreath (3-inch-diameter) or other small wreath; small pinecone; small gold jingle bell; 8-inch length of 1/2-inch-wide red satin ribbon; 8-inch length of gold tinsel; hot glue gun; candle.

Directions: Keeping cellophane wrappers intact, glue candy canes around PVC pipe with straight ends of canes even with one end of pipe. Make sure cane hooks are level on bottom, so candle holder will sit level.

Hot-glue candy wreath to front of candle holder. Glue small pinecone to bottom of wreath. Make a small bow from satin ribbon and attach it to candy wreath beneath pinecone. Hot-glue bell to center of bow.

Wrap gold tinsel around top of holder, anchoring with a dot of glue in three or four places. Place candle in holder, being careful not to press down too hard. ✷

CREATE A CLASSY CARDIGAN

WHAT BETTER way to express warm feelings—and to keep a loved one warm—than to create cozy, classic garments like this one for Christmas?

GIRL'S KNIT CARDIGAN

Materials needed: Bernat Sesame "4", a 100% virgin wool worsted-weight yarn in 100-gram skeins with about 220 yards per skein—2(3,3,4) skeins of Banana No. 7500; straight knitting needles and 24-inch circular needles, both in sizes 5 and 7 (or sizes needed for correct gauge); 1 skein each of red and green tapestry wool; 6(7,7,7) 1/2-inch buttons; two stitch holders; stitch markers; size 18 tapestry needle.

Finished size: Directions are given for size 4 (24 inches). Changes for sizes 6 (26 inches), 8 (28 inches) and 10 (30 inches) are given in parentheses.

Gauge: 4.75 sts = 1 inch when worked in stockinette st (k 1 row, p 1 row) on size 7 needles. Always check gauge before starting project.

Directions:
Body: Body is worked in one piece to armhole. With size 5 circular needle, cast on 100(106,118,124) sts. Working back and forth in rows, not rnds, * k 1, p 1; repeat from * across row. Repeat last row until rib measures 1-1/2 inches. Evenly space 12 incs on last row of rib so there are 112 (118,130,136) sts. Change to size 7 circular needle and begin pattern.
Pattern row 1: * P 4, k 2; repeat from * across; end p 4.
Pattern row 2: * K 4, p 2; repeat from * across; end k 4.
Pattern row 3: Repeat row 1.
Pattern row 4: Purl.
Pattern row 5: P 1; * k 2, p 4; repeat from * across; end k 2, p 1.
Pattern row 6: K 1; * p 2, k 4; repeat from * across; end p 2, k 1.
Pattern row 7: Repeat row 5.
Pattern row 8: Purl.

Repeat rows 1 through 8 until piece measures 9-1/2 (10,10-1/2,11) inches above cast-on row. End with either a row 4 or a row 8 of pattern.

Next row: With front of garment facing, p 23(25,28,29) sts; bind off 6 sts; p 54(56,62, 66) sts; bind off 6 sts; p to end of row and leave all sts on needle.

Sleeves: With size 5 straight needles, cast on 26(28,30,32) sts. Work in k 1, p 1 rib for 1-1/2 inches. Evenly space 8(6,10,8) incs on last row of rib so there are 34(34,40,40) sts.

Change to size 7 needles and work in pattern as established for body of garment. Inc 1 st each end of work every eighth row 7(8,6,7) times. Adjust the way

each row begins and ends so all sts remain in pattern.

Work even on 48(50,52,54) sts until sleeve measures 11(12,13,14) inches above cast-on row. End with either a pattern row 4 or a pattern row 4 or a pattern row 8. With right side facing, bind off 4(4,3,3) sts; p to within last 4(4,3,3) sts and bind off these last sts. Break yarn and place these sts on a holder. Make second sleeve in same manner. Break yarn and leave second sleeve on needle.

Yoke: With wrong side of garment facing, purl across sts for body on circular needle to first 6 bound-off sts; place marker; purl across sleeve sts that are on straight needle so they are now on circular needle; place marker; purl across back section to next 6 bound-off sts; place marker; purl across sleeve sts that are on holder so they are now on circular needle; place marker; purl to end of row. Purl to end of row. Purl two more rows across these 180(190,210, 220) sts, slipping markers from one needle to the next as you work.

Raglan shaping: With right side of garment facing, * knit to within 2 sts of first marker; k 2 tog, slip marker, sl 2 sts knit-wise, insert left-hand needle in front of these 2 sts from left to right and k 2 tog; repeat from * three times, then knit to end of row. Purl 1 row. Repeat these 2 rows for shaping. At same time, when yoke measures 2-3/4(3-1/4, 3-3/4,4) inches, place first 3 sts on holder at beg of next 2 rows; then dec 1 st each end every other row 1(2,3,4) times. Continue raglan shaping until 36(36,38,38) sts remain. Leave sts on needle and break yarn.

Neckband: With size 5 needles and right side of garment facing, work across 3 sts from first front holder; pick up and k 5 sts on side of neck; work across 36(36,38,38) sts from circular needle; pick up and k 5 sts on

side of neck; work across 3 sts from second front holder. Work on these 52(52,54,54) sts in k 1, p 1 rib for 1 inch. Bind off all sts in rib.

Front band: With size 5 needles and right side facing, pick up and k 76(80,86,90) sts on left edge of front. Work in k 1, p 1 rib for 1 inch. Bind off all sts in rib.

Work right-hand edge in same manner, but at same time evenly space 6(7, 7,7) 1-stitch buttonholes (yo, k 2 tog) in center of band. Begin and end buttonholes 1/2 inch from top and bottom edges.

Finishing: Sew underarm and sleeve seams. Sew buttons opposite buttonholes. Use tapestry needle to embroider flowers. See Fig. 1 for placement. Use red tapestry yarn to work flowers in lazy daisy stitch. Add green leaves in straight stitch.❊

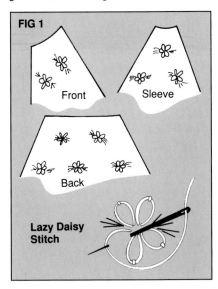

FIG 1

Front Sleeve

Back

Lazy Daisy Stitch

FASHION THAT'S FUN AND FAST

WRAP UP a simple-to-decorate sweatshirt that will make your bicycle-loving girl or boy jump for joy. All it takes is a hot iron on adhesive webbing to attach the checkered bandana, and fabric paints to create the rainbow of bikes. You can have it finished in no time flat!

BICYCLE SWEATSHIRT

Materials needed: Bicycle pattern; red sweatshirt; one black/white checked bandana or 1/8 yard fabric with 1-inch black/white checks; Tulip Slick Paints—black, yellow, white and blue; 1/8 yard paper-backed fusible webbing; iron; dressmaker's tracing paper; T-shirt board (or piece of cardboard that fits inside sweatshirt covered with a plastic garbage bag); paper towels.

Note: For more sweatshirt designs, two books are available: No. 247, *Fun with Bandanas* and No. 248, *Bunches of Bandanas*. For each book, send check for $5 plus $1 postage and handling to Kappie Originals, 801 East St., Frederick MD 21701. Make sure you mention the book numbers and titles.

Directions: Wash and dry sweatshirt to remove sizing. Do not use fabric softener or stain-resistant detergents—these could cause paints to wash out.

Cut bandana or checked fabric into 2-inch-wide strips. Cut one strip to fit across front width of sweatshirt and two strips to fit around sleeves, above elbow area. Following manufacturer's instructions, fuse webbing to back of strips. Remove paper backing and fuse strips to sweatshirt, placing front strip about 4 inches up from bottom ribbing. Adjust placement on smaller shirts if necessary.

Place T-shirt board inside sweatshirt to prevent paint from bleeding through to back. Practice squeezing an even line of paint on a paper towel, then use tip of paint bottle to outline fabric edges with black paint. Let dry.

Use dressmaker's tracing paper to transfer bicycle pattern to shirt, evenly repeating pattern across front with wheels overlapping. Shirt shown has four repeats. Smaller shirts may require fewer repeats. Refer to photo for help with placement.

Use tip of paint bottle to paint bicycles. Do not overlap paints where tires overlap (see photo). Working from right to left, paint first bicycle white, second one blue, third one yellow and last one black.

Lay shirt flat to dry for about 4 hours. Paints should "cure" for 7 days before washing. To machine-wash, turn garment inside out and wash and rinse in warm water on gentle cycle with a mild detergent.✳

BICYCLE SWEATSHIRT

A GESTURE FROM THE HEART

BY GRACE SMITH, ST. PETERSBURG, FLORIDA

My father was a minister in a small church in Pontiac, Michigan, and one of our Christmas "duties" was the delivery of Christmas baskets of food for poorer families.

In addition to preparing the baskets, Mother and other women from the church collected gifts such as games and toys that would be delivered with the baskets.

A couple of weeks before Christmas, Mother asked me if I'd like to participate in the "giving" portion of the Christmas basket delivery. She suggested I find the one toy that had given me the most pleasure.

That did not take much time or thought, as my favorite toy had been the doll one of the members of the congregation had given me. My doll had gone everywhere with me: to Sunday school, church, grocery shopping with Mother, picnics and potlucks.

Since she'd been given to me at Christmas, I'd named her "Chrissie". For sure, Chrissie had been my constant companion, but as I looked at her I really wondered whether she could make another child happy.

Her hair was matted, her dress and bonnet soiled, and her arms and legs were dirty. Still, Chrissie had given me so much joy!

Mother offered to wash and iron her dress and bonnet while I scrubbed her arms and legs, whitened her shoes with shoe polish and brushed her hair into ringlets that poked out nicely under her bonnet. When we finished, Chrissie looked like new!

Finally, Christmas Eve arrived and it was time for the delivery of baskets and gifts. I

"I really wondered whether my doll could make another child happy."

squished into the backseat of the car, which was loaded with Christmas packages, and held Chrissie in my lap.

It was wonderful to see the expressions of gratitude on the faces of the families receiving their gifts. At last, there was only one more basket left to deliver. Mother and Father said I could accompany them to the little apartment above a garage where the last family lived.

There were two boys and a little girl. I was told that this would be Chrissie's new home. As we climbed the stairs to the apartment, Father carried the heavy food basket, Mother carried two wrapped gifts and I had Chrissie in my arms.

When we entered the apartment, I was surprised to see no Christmas tree. A table decorated with holly branches was the only sign of the season. Father put the basket in the small kitchen, and Mother placed the two gifts on the table next to the holly branches.

I saw the little girl looking with longing eyes at Chrissie, so I handed her the doll. With one arm around

Chrissie and the other wrapped around my neck, she planted a kiss on my cheek.

Tears were in her eyes, as well as those of the adults looking on, as she said, "This is the first doll I have ever had. Thank you so very much!"

For all of my life I've remembered the Christmas Eve that I helped make a little girl so happy. That night I learned a lesson I could never forget: It really *is* more blessed to give than to receive!

How I Spent My
'CHRISTMAS QUARTER'

BY KATHRYN MCGAUGHEY, DENVER, COLORADO

My mother was a genius at "making-do" during the Depression. It was a happy time for us children, and we were never aware that we were missing out on anything.

One Christmas my mother somehow managed to spare a shiny quarter and gave it to me to buy gifts. I was ecstatic! Twenty-five whole cents—more money than I'd ever seen! I put it inside my wool mitten. I clasped and unclasped it, feeling its power.

I wandered through the aisles of the five-and-dime, wondering what to buy. Amid a display of hair ribbons and bobby pins, I found two beautiful red bone clips for 5¢; they'd look beautiful in Sis' black hair!

Next I walked through the sewing department, looking carefully at all the yardage. Then I spied a rack of thimbles. With all Mother's quilting, mending and darning, her old thimble was worn and thin. I gave the clerk a dime for one, and got a nickel in change.

Dad was next, and his gift was easy. He loved licorice; that would tickle his sweet tooth all morning! I bought 10 strings of it at a penny each.

I still had a nickel left. What could I buy for myself? A double-dip ice cream cone? Maybe a candy bar?

But then my conscience told me I was very lucky to have a whole quarter to spend for Christmas gifts, since so many people had needs greater than mine. Our minister had told us all about world hunger, and I knew my nickel could help a lot.

So, come Sunday morning, I dropped my prized nickel into the collection plate. I felt as generous as a great philanthropist!

Today we spend more than a quarter just to mail a letter, and I think nothing of spending $25 on a gift. But I doubt any shopping spree will ever compare to that Depression-era Christmas, when my mother gave me a *whole quarter*.

THE STRANGER'S GIFT

BY GENEVIEVE BRANDON, STERLING, ILLINOIS

The December day was bleak, just as every day from mid-September on had been that cheerless winter of 1932. The cold weather had settled in early, wiping out the fall crop of vegetables.

Over our small village in northwestern Illinois, as over all the nation, there hung an aura of quiet desperation. These were the deepest, darkest days of the Depression. With so many people out of work, there seemed to be little to look forward to this holiday season.

My husband and I huddled close to the heating stove that morning, rationing the cheap coal and trying to suppress our dreams of a joyful Christmas for our three small children. Suddenly, there was a knock.

When I opened the door I found a poorly clad, shivering stranger standing there. He was holding a small Christmas tree, and, in the background behind him, I could see a rusty old truck loaded with cut trees.

"Buy a tree, lady?" he asked hopefully. "They're just 25¢."

Price Was Too Steep

Sadly, I shook my head, with tears welling up. "No," I answered, "I haven't got a quarter in the house."

So the stranger left and went elsewhere to peddle his trees, leaving me dejected and hopeless and despising myself because we didn't have even 25¢ to spend to bring a little pleasure into our drab surroundings.

That evening, there again came a rapping on our door.

When I opened it, the same wearied stranger stood there, one scrawny tree in his hand.

"Take this," he said. "It's the only one I have left. No one wanted it—it's twisted and one side is nearly bare, but if you put it in a corner it will look all right."

Charity? "No, I am not a beggar," I started to say icily, but before I could get all the words out, I was stopped by his eyes.

A Plea from the Heart

They were silently pleading, begging me to accept his gift, if not for me, then for the children—*and* for him. With a sudden change of heart, I reached out and took the sickly looking tree and murmured, "Thank you."

"No," he said, quietly echoing my words, "thank *you*."

I invited him in out of the cold, and after a hot cup of coffee, he stood up, adjusted his earflaps and disappeared back out into the night. We never saw him again.

A little thing? Perhaps. Then again, I had the feeling it was the only Christmas gesture that poor man was capable of that doleful year. But, for both of us, that one little act of kindness brought a priceless measure of the peace and joy engendered in a lonely stable in a far-off land almost 2,000 years ago.

For 60 years now, I've thought of that dear stranger every holiday season. And, every year, out over the clear, crisp air, I've sent a silent prayer of hope that all his Christmases since have been filled with joy and love and cheer.

Homemakers' Holiday Project
SHINES WITH SEASON'S SPIRIT

When the Extension Homemakers of Greenup County, Kentucky get set for Christmas, they don't think small! Banding together, the women turn out some 500 ornaments—enough to decorate a 14-ft.-tall tree. Plus, they produce 16 smaller special trees.

The reason is equally as impressive...proving once again the true spirit of the holidays is not in getting but in giving.

These Homemakers don't do that ambitious decorating at home. Every year, beginning in August, they train their talents on Greenbo Lake State Park Lodge—transforming the rustic building into a winter wonderland all can enjoy.

"Each woman makes an ornament for the large tree in the lobby," notes Ruby Mauk, a farm woman from Murray, who helped originate the public-spirited project 7 years ago. "We work 2 full days trimming that tree and the others, hanging garlands and putting up decorations. It's a lot of work...but we have fun, too!

Each holiday season, the Homemakers look forward to sharing crafting skills and enjoying each other's company. "Over the years, we've learned from each other —how to make bows, cornshuck dolls, tatted and crocheted ornaments. Best of all, we've gotten to know each other in the process."

When they're done decorating, the Homemakers hold an open house at the lodge, featuring an old-fashioned "groaning board" of holiday food.

Then, throughout the season, their combined effort brightens the many Christmas parties, dinners and weddings that the lodge hosts, and produces many merry memories for all!

FOR KIDS FROM 1 TO 92.
These Extension Homemakers make local state park lodge sparkle every holiday season. At far left, Ruby Mauk (middle) helps trim festive fireplace…then (top left) works on shimmering tree set against colorful quilt. Volunteer decorators like those above lend lots of imagination to annual undertaking—resulting in eye-pleasing "theme" trees such as sunbonnet one (top right), western-flavored example (left) and red and white gingham beauty (bottom left).

Across the Miles...
MY CHERUB SMILED

BY ROXANA CHALMERS, SEDALIA, COLORADO

With the final tiny stitch finished, Elsie snipped the pink thread. Smiling, she held the soft-stuffed Christmas tree ornament at arms' length. Then she sighed. She had planned to make an *elegant* angel—but instead, had ended up with a fat little cherub. Elsie could just imagine what her daughter's reaction would be. "Oh, Mom," she could hear Ginny say, "if that isn't just like you!"

Maybe, Elsie mused, she should try to make another. If only there were time! Why couldn't she have thought of the idea sooner?

The idea wouldn't have occurred to her at all if she hadn't been sorting fabric scraps that morning. From her box of white materials, Elsie had pulled a plastic bag filled with remnants from Ginny's wedding dress—handfuls of satin and lace.

Her discovery had brought on a new wave of loneliness for her daughter. In a whirlwind summer, Ginny and her fiance, Mike, had graduated from medical school, gotten married and, immediately after the wedding, moved to Boston to begin their internships at the same hospital. This would be Ginny's first Christmas away from the Midwest farm where she'd grown up.

Opening the bag of wedding scraps, and sliding the smooth, cool satin through her fingers, Elsie had a sudden inspiration to make an angel from the remnants for the young couple's first Christmas tree. True, it was exactly the kind of sweet sentimentality Ginny would scoff at. But even an aluminum tree needs an angel for its top, Elsie decided! Besides, maybe she could create one with a modern look more to Ginny's liking.

Her angel, however, had none of the abstract style that Ginny adored. His blushing full cheeks and rosy lips were childlike, and his gleaming folds and flounces embellished with lace looked like fanciful clothes for a doll. Oh well…Elsie decided to pack it in the Christmas box anyway. At least it would give Ginny a chuckle.

Christmas Day soon arrived, and the family clustered around the phone taking turns talking to Ginny. As they chattered and laughed, Elsie scurried about the kitchen, checking pots that didn't need checking. Each time someone offered her the receiver, she waved it away.

Finally, though, her turn came—just as she was adjusting a cluster of bells hanging from the curtains…and noting the chipped silver coating. She could almost hear Ginny: "You're not putting those old things up again, are you?"

But the voice on the other end of the telephone caught her off guard with its enthusiasm. "It's so great talking to everyone!" Ginny bubbled. "I feel as if I'm right there with you!

"We'll be going next door for Christmas dinner soon. They're such a nice old couple. You'd really like them, Mom. And last night Mike and I helped with a party in the children's ward at the hospital. It's sad they couldn't go home, but I think they had fun."

Ginny paused. Elsie swallowed hard and finally managed to say, "What a lovely way for Mike and you to spend your Christmas."

"Oh, it's not as wonderful as being home," Ginny answered quietly. Then her voice picked up. "Thanks for the great Christmas parcel! We took the cookies to the hospital party. And we love the shirts. What a terrific idea, Mom—matching wool shirts!"

Ginny chatted happily about the other gifts from her family. But she didn't mention the angel. Elsie imagined it tucked away in a drawer…

It was a month later that Elsie pulled a thick envelope from the mailbox. Pictures from Ginny! She hurried inside and settled herself in an overstuffed chair.

Inside there was a letter…Elsie grinned at Ginny's firm vertical handwriting. And there were also photos of the Christmas party at the hospital: children in bed clutching gifts, Ginny holding a small girl wearing a cast, Mike in a Santa suit.

Elsie lingered over them. It hadn't been a traditional Christmas her daughter had celebrated, true, she thought. Still, that was part of growing up—growing apart and finding your own way.

So, when she came to the final picture in the pile, Elsie was surprised to feel a lump forming in her throat.

There, wearing the new wool shirts she had sent them, were Ginny and Mike…sitting in front of a tinsel-draped, potted Norfolk pine. And there, at the very top, pulling the tree slightly askew, was her own fat little cherub smiling back at her!

A TOUCH OF GLASS

NOW YOU can help an angel get its wings, as well as a prominent spot at the top of your tree. And don't forget the beautiful bell. Both are glistening stained glass ornaments that will add beauty to any bough.

STAINED GLASS BELL AND TREETOP ANGEL

Materials needed: Patterns; tracing or pattern paper; pencil; carbon paper; glass cutter; grozing pliers; grinding stone or electric grinder; 7/32-inch copper foil; flux and flux brush; 63/37 solder; soldering iron; small length of pre-tinned copper wire and wire cutters; non-scratching scouring powder and old toothbrush; solder patina; small paintbrush or cotton swabs; glass polishing compound.

FOR BELL: Green cathedral and whispy white opalescent stained glass; 18 inches of 1/8-inch-wide green satin ribbon.

FOR TREETOP ANGEL: Solid white opalescent, solid yellow-gold opalescent, whispy peach opalescent and red hammered cathedral stained glass; night-light clamp.

Directions: Trace all patterns to tracing paper but do not cut out. Following color guide on patterns and using carbon paper, with transfer side on right side of glass, transfer pattern sections to appropriate glass pieces. Smooth side of glass is right side, except for angel, which uses red hammered cathedral glass wrong (textured) side up. Using glass cutter, score pattern lines. Break off excess glass beyond pattern lines with grozing pliers. Once all cuts have been made, sand all edges smooth with grinding stone or electric grinder. Wipe glass clean.

Wrap all edges of each piece with copper foil, making sure to overlap evenly on front and back. Lap foil ends for about 1/4 inch. Place all pieces, right side up, on their respective patterns. Using flux brush, apply flux to foil. Using pre-heated soldering iron, apply solder to join pieces. Apply thin layer of solder along outside edges and turn pieces right side down. Apply solder to all back seams. For ornament hanger, cut a small length of pre-tinned copper wire and shape it into a small ring or loop. Solder to ornament where indicated on pattern. For angel, cut length of pre-tinned copper wire and shape into halo. Solder to angel where indicated on pattern. Solder night-light clamp to back of angel where indicated on pattern.

With paintbrush or cotton swab, apply patina to solder where desired. Polish finished piece with glass polishing compound. Attach green satin ribbon to ornament hanger.❈

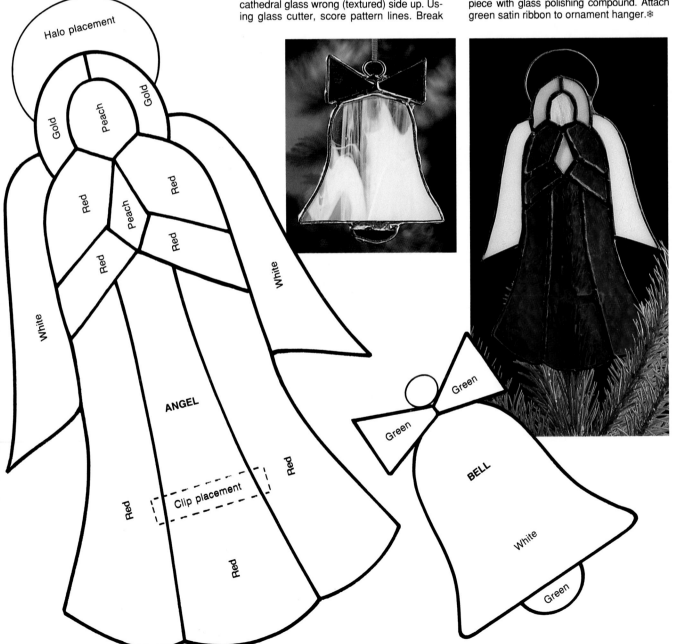

CALICO CHRISTMAS TRIMS

YOU CAN use ribbon a completely different way when you cover simple wood shapes with calico ribbon woven back and forth.

WOVEN RIBBON WOOD ORNAMENTS

Materials needed: Ribbon—9 inches per ornament of 1/16-inch double-faced satin ribbon for hanging loop, 5/8 yard per ornament of No. 5 cotton print ribbon in color of your choice, 5/8 yard in contrasting color; pattern below, 1/4-inch plywood and scroll saw or precut wood shapes of your choice, no larger than 3 x 3 inches; seven pushpins; tacky glue; water-base gloss finish; craft knife with sharp No. 11 blade; pieces of foamcore or homosote board.

Directions: Cut each piece of print ribbon into four equal lengths. Cut each of these pieces in half lengthwise. With wrong sides up, pin seven strips of one color ribbon side by side onto foamcore board. Place pins at top, short end of each piece.

With wrong side up, weave a length of second color over and under pinned strips. Weave next length of second color under and over pinned strips. Continue in this manner for eight rows. Ribbons should butt up against one another.

Use favorite method to transfer pattern below to plywood. Use sabre saw to cut shape or use precut wood shape. Spread tacky glue over the surface of one side. Place glued side on top of woven ribbons. Allow glue to dry. Remove pushpins. Trim ribbon around wooden shape with craft knife. Glue edge pieces where necessary.

Apply three coats of gloss finish to ribbons. Allow to dry between coats. Fold satin ribbon in half and glue cut edges to back of wood shape 1/2 inch below top edge to form hanging loop.✻

A CHOIR OF ANGELS

CAPTURE THE sparkle and spirit of the season with pretty pastel angel ornaments that are a breeze to make. You'll find the angels go quickest when you make several at once.

BARNWOOD ANGELS

Materials needed: Patterns on page 69; transfer paper; pencil; 8-inch length of 8-inch-wide x 3/4-inch- or 5/8-inch-thick barnwood or pine lumber for each angel; scrap of 3/8-inch-thick pine lumber; scrap of 1/4-inch-thick birch; scroll or band saw; small stiff scrub brush; sandpaper; tack cloth; medium-weight jute; tacks or staples, No. 5 double point; hammer; 18-inch lengths of 1/8-inch-wide satin ribbon in colors that coordinate with paints; 8-inch-wide paper twist—blue, rose and red (4-inch-wide twist can be substituted); stapler; wood glue; hot glue gun; flat 3/8-inch or 1/2-inch paintbrush; stiff toothbrush; Folk Art acrylic paints—Flesh, Slate Blue, Rose Garden, Ivory, Huckleberry and Black; Illinois Bronze acrylic paint—Mushroom; walnut acrylic wood stain; Spanish moss.

Finished size: Angel measures 8 inches tall x 10 inches wide.

Directions: Angels shown were made with 5/8-inch-thick barnwood. If your barnwood has some paint on it, leave it on. Brush old wood with dry scrub brush to remove all dust and dirt.

To age new wood, lightly rub it with a small amount of Mushroom paint. Do not attempt to cover wood completely. Practice on a scrap of wood.

Transfer patterns to wood. Cut out all pieces. Sand pieces very lightly, leaving front of barnwood unsanded. Remove sanding dust with tack cloth.

Paint all faces Flesh. Paint front of bodies and arms either Ivory, Slate Blue or Rose Garden, leaving the edges unpainted. Paint pink angel's heart Dusty Rose and remaining angels' hearts Huckleberry, painting front and edges of each heart. Sand off any paint that may have run over the edges of bodies and arms.

If new wood is being used, stain back and edges of bodies and arms, leaving top edge of head where Spanish moss will be glued unstained. Leave barnwood angels unstained.

Cut a 27-inch length of jute for each angel. Tack or staple jute to back of angles as shown on pattern, then tie a bow about 3 inches above each angel's head.

Attach arm pieces with wood glue. See pattern for placement. To spatter angels with Black paint, dip bristles of toothbrush in paint, then while holding brush 2 to 3 inches from wood, point bristles toward wood and move index finger over bristles toward yourself to create spatters. Practice this technique on wood scraps or newspaper before spattering angels. Let dry. Glue hearts in place.

To make wings, cut one 20-inch length

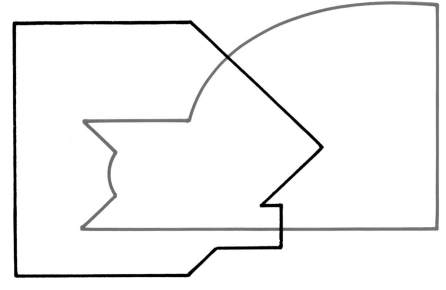

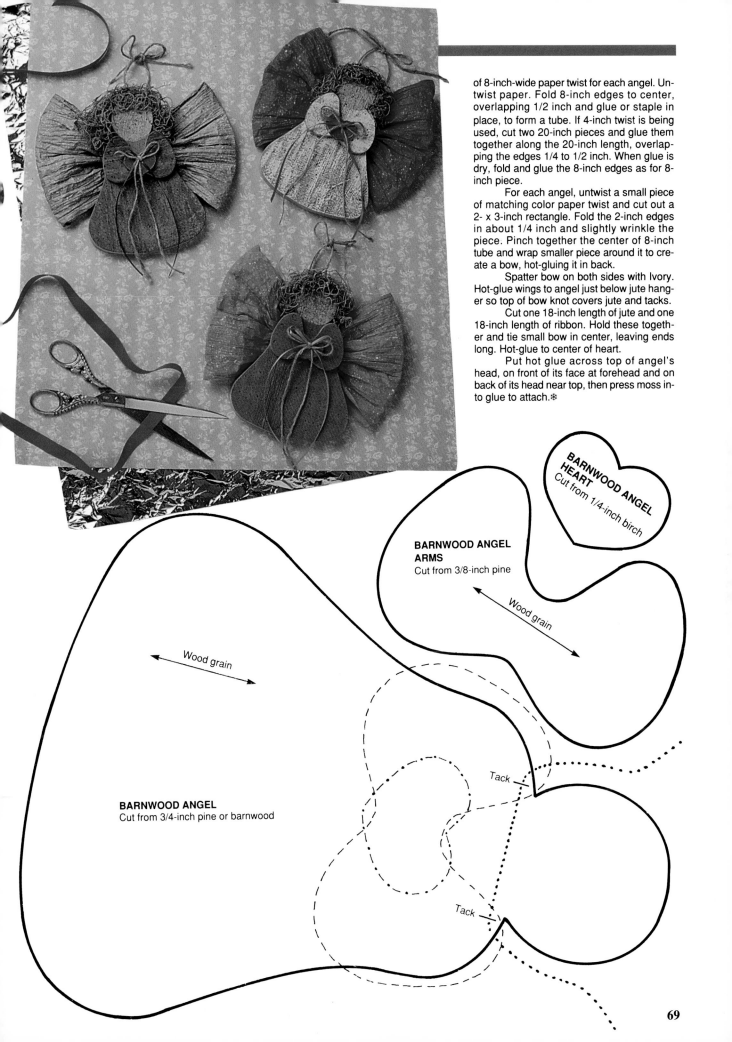

of 8-inch-wide paper twist for each angel. Untwist paper. Fold 8-inch edges to center, overlapping 1/2 inch and glue or staple in place, to form a tube. If 4-inch twist is being used, cut two 20-inch pieces and glue them together along the 20-inch length, overlapping the edges 1/4 to 1/2 inch. When glue is dry, fold and glue the 8-inch edges as for 8-inch piece.

For each angel, untwist a small piece of matching color paper twist and cut out a 2- x 3-inch rectangle. Fold the 2-inch edges in about 1/4 inch and slightly wrinkle the piece. Pinch together the center of 8-inch tube and wrap smaller piece around it to create a bow, hot-gluing it in back.

Spatter bow on both sides with Ivory. Hot-glue wings to angel just below jute hanger so top of bow knot covers jute and tacks.

Cut one 18-inch length of jute and one 18-inch length of ribbon. Hold these together and tie small bow in center, leaving ends long. Hot-glue to center of heart.

Put hot glue across top of angel's head, on front of its face at forehead and on back of its head near top, then press moss into glue to attach.✻

BARNWOOD ANGEL HEART
Cut from 1/4-inch birch

BARNWOOD ANGEL ARMS
Cut from 3/8-inch pine

Wood grain

Wood grain

BARNWOOD ANGEL
Cut from 3/4-inch pine or barnwood

Tack

Tack

CORRAL SOME CHRISTMAS CRITTERS

ADD A little country to your Christmas tree by sewing up some adorable animal ornaments. These fun-to-make farmyard friends are even more endearing because you can use leftover scraps of fabric, muslin and ribbon to make them!

BARNYARD ORNAMENTS

Materials needed: Patterns; tracing paper; pencil; 1/8 yard or scraps of muslin; 1/8 yard or scraps of two or more coordinating fabrics for clothing; small scrap of sherpa for lamb; small scraps of 1/8-inch ribbon in colors that coordinate with fabrics; black and dark pink acrylic craft paints; artist's brushes—fine liner, and either a dry brush or No. 4 stencil brush; hot glue gun; small amount of polyester stuffing; tiny cowbell; small crochet hook; standard painting and sewing supplies.

Directions: Trace patterns to tracing paper and cut out. Fold muslin in half, wrong sides together. Place head, arm, leg, body and ear patterns on doubled muslin and trace around each shape with pencil, spacing them at least 1/4 inch apart. Trace body pattern once for each animal. Trace legs and arms twice for each animal. Do NOT cut the muslin yet. Sew on traced lines, leaving small openings where indicated on patterns by short broken lines. The heads have no openings.

Cut out muslin pieces, leaving a 1/8-inch seam all around. For heads, carefully pull apart two layers of fabric and cut a small slash near bottom edge of one layer for turning. Use crochet hook as an aid to turn heads right side out through slashes and remaining pieces right side out through openings.

Fill all but ears with stuffing. Neatly hand-sew slashes on heads closed. Turn in raw edges on remaining pieces and sew closed. Hand-stitch arms and legs to bodies. Position heads so they overlap bodies as shown on pattern, hiding slashes. Hand-sew heads in place. Fold bottom edge of each ear in half and sew to appropriate head.

Cut one pig snout from muslin and sew a gathering line 1/8 inch from edge. Pull thread to gather, forming a small pouch. Tuck a tiny amount of stuffing in snout and neatly hand-sew to pig's face.

Painting: Using patterns as a guide, paint spots and horns on cow and all hoofs black. Paint two small dots on each animal for eyes, adding lashes on cow and pig. Paint a fine black line under nose of lamb and bunny, adding a small curve on each side of line for mouth. Paint a larger curved black line on cow and pig for mouth. Open up ears to shade inside with pink, using a small stencil brush or dry brush. Finally dry-brush a small circle of pink on each cheek.

Clothing: Fold print fabrics in half, wrong sides together. Place clothing patterns on doubled fabrics and trace around each shape once for each animal, spacing them at least 1/4 inch apart. Sew on traced lines, leaving open where marked on pattern by short broken lines. Cut out, leaving a 1/8-inch seam. Clip corners. Turn right side out.

Turn under upper edge of bloomers and hand-sew a line of gathers, pulling gathers to fit waist of animal. Turn under raw edges at leg openings and sew gathers to fit legs.

Turn under bottom edge of dress and hand-sew in place with running stitches. Place dress on animal and turn under neck edge. Sew gathering line along neck edge

and pull gathers to fit neck. Secure neckline with a few stitches. Turn under raw edge of each sleeve and gather to fit around arms.

Finishing: Trace sherpa pattern from top of lamb's head pattern and cut out. Place pattern on back of sherpa and cut through backing fabric. Hand-sew to head, folding top edge over just enough to cover top seam. Hot-glue a tiny bow to fleece (see photo).

Hot-glue a tiny bow to cow's horn. Thread cowbell on a small piece of ribbon, tie a bow and hot-glue bow just below cow's neck. Hot-glue bows below neckline of remaining animals.✳

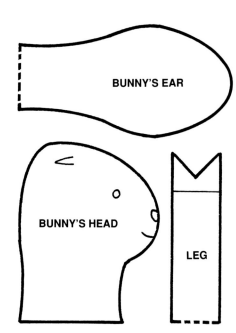

BUNNY'S EAR

BUNNY'S HEAD

LEG

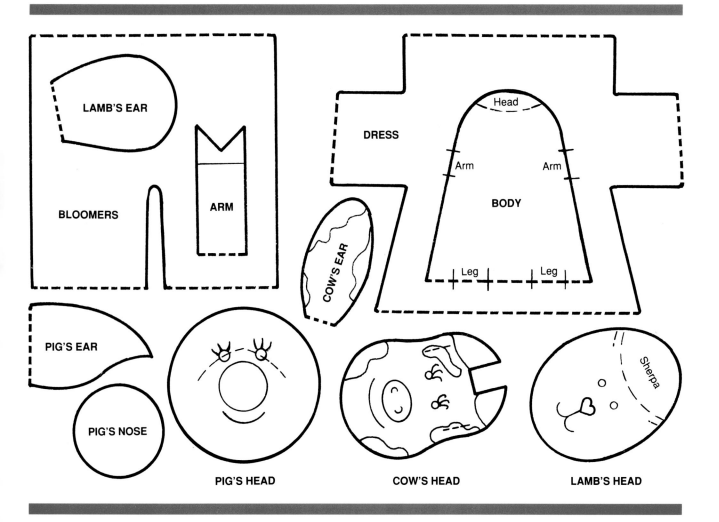

LAMB'S EAR

BLOOMERS

ARM

DRESS

Head

Arm   Arm

BODY

COW'S EAR

Leg   Leg

PIG'S EAR

PIG'S NOSE

PIG'S HEAD

COW'S HEAD

Sherpa

LAMB'S HEAD

CRAFT A CUTE SANTA...FROM YOUR GARDEN!

YOU CAN turn an ordinary gourd into an extraordinary ornament with a little paint and some red cord! Plus, it's a quick and easy project the whole family can enjoy.

GOURD SANTA

Materials needed: Small dried gourd; red spray paint; acrylic craft paints—white, peach, red and black; clear acrylic spray finish; small stencil brushes; small artist's brush; drill with 1/32-inch bit; tack cloth; small piece of thin wire; 7 inches of red cord for hanging; fine grit sandpaper; paper towels.

Directions: Clean surface of gourd with fine grit sandpaper. Drill holes through top of gourd to accommodate cord for hanging. Use tack cloth to remove dirt and dust. Thread gourd on a piece of wire so it hangs free when spray-painting. Working in a well-ventilated area and protecting surrounding area from over spray, spray entire gourd with red

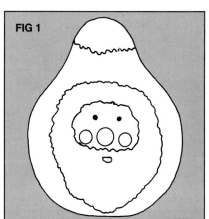

FIG 1

paint, using several light coats for nice coverage. Let dry thoroughly.

When dry, refer to Fig. 1 and paint Santa's face using stencil brush and peach paint, working as follows: Dip brush into paint and pounce brush on newspaper or paper towel to remove excess paint. Apply paint to gourd in a dabbing motion. When face is dry, add white around face for hair and beard and hat top. Add red cheeks and nose. Paint mouth with artist's brush and red paint. Use end of artist's brush dipped in black to make dots for eyes. Let dry. Spray entire gourd with several coats of clear acrylic finish. When dry, remove from wire and hang from red cord.✳

THIMBLE BELLS ARE RINGING SUCCESSES

MOST FOLKS "wood" feel proud to hang one of these bells on a tree. Hand-painted wooden thimble bells are a hit on boughs and at bazaars.

THIMBLE BELLS

Materials needed: Wooden thimbles (see note below); gold metallic thread; 3/32- x 12-inch piece of brass tubing (sold in hobby shops)—12-inch piece is enough for 12 bells; craft knife with No. 11 blade; one 5mm pearl bead per bell; acrylic paints or metal enamel paints; a variety of artist's brushes; a variety of ribbon, lace and metallic trims; clear-drying white glue or tacky glue; a flat toothpick; waxed paper; drill with a 1/16-inch bit; glossy spray varnish or urethane; scissors; pencil.

Note: Wooden thimbles are available from Technicraft, Box 217, Dept. CH, Auburn MA 01501 (catalog is $1, refundable with first order). Brass tubing used for the clappers is available from Whittemore-Durgin Glass Co., Box 2065, Dept. CH, Hanover MA 02339 (catalog is $1).

Directions: To make clapper for bell, use pencil or craft knife to mark off a 1-inch length of tubing. Score the tubing deeply at marked point with craft knife. Snap off tubing at 1-inch mark.

Cut a 12-inch length of metallic thread. Thread single strand through pearl, then tube. Fold strand in half and thread end back through tube and pearl. Folded end should stick out of tube at top. See Fig. 1.

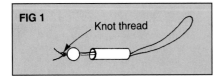

FIG 1 Knot thread

Tie two loose ends together at bottom of pearl and trim off any excess thread to within 1/4 inch of knot. Use toothpick to apply a small dab of white glue to knot.

Drill a hole through top of thimble. Bell can be left natural or can be painted a solid color before adding design. Allow paint to dry before adding details. Details are painted freehand. Use Fig. 2 and photo as guide or create your own designs. If preferred, glue various ribbon and metallic trims to thimbles instead.

Follow manufacturer's directions to apply one or two light coats of glossy spray varnish or urethane.

From inside of thimble, insert folded end of clapper's thread through drilled hole. Gently pull on thread until clapper is snug inside bell. Use toothpick to apply a small dab of glue to outer surface of bell at point where thread passes through hole. White glue will dry clear. Hang ornament until glue is dry.❈

FIG 2

LITTLE DRUMMER 'TOYS'

YOU CAN dress up your tree or drum up a little more business at your local craft fair this holiday season with these ornaments.

DRUM ORNAMENTS

Materials needed: 6-ounce orange juice (or lemonade) can with pull strip; gold spray paint; 7-1/2 inches of 7/8-inch-wide plaid ribbon; 13 inches of 1/8-inch-wide gold flat braid or narrow rickrack; 12 small (1/4-inch) red or green pom-poms; two round toothpicks; 10 inches of gold thread; hot glue gun.

Directions: Carefully open juice can so lid isn't damaged. Set lid aside. Remove contents, then rinse and dry can well. Measure and mark a line around can, 1 inch from bottom. Cut along line. Replace top lid on "shortened" can.

Spray top and bottom lids with gold paint. When dry, glue plaid ribbon around can. Mark six equal sections, approximately 1-1/8 inches apart, around top edge of can, and then do the same around the bottom edge, spacing these marks halfway between top marks.

Glue one end of gold braid to first top mark, then angle down to bottom mark, fold over and up to second top mark, and so forth to end. Glue pom-pom at each point of braid. Attach gold thread through braid for hanger. Glue toothpicks on top of drum.❈

CRAFT SOME SANTAS... JUST BECLAUS!

THESE Humpty Dumpty look-alikes fit right into your holiday decor when dressed up as Santas, whether they hang from a Christmas tree or sit on a wall or mantel. Be creative and don't worry—they're made of wooden eggs so they're unlikely to break!

EGGHEAD SANTAS

Materials needed: One medium-size wooden egg; two 2-1/2-inch-long chunky mini shelf pegs for legs; two 1-3/4-inch-long mini shelf pegs for arms; nine 1/2-inch metal eye screws; small hand saw or scroll saw; drill with 1/16-inch bit; sandpaper; needle-nose pliers; artist's brushes—No. 6 flat, No. 0 or No. 1 liner for detailing, No. 2 or No. 4 round for basecoating; Delta Ceramcoat acrylic paints—Fire Red, Black, Christmas Green, Salem Green, Flesh and Coral; water-base varnish; gesso; 1/2 yard of 1/8- or 1/16-inch ribbon (optional); standard painting supplies.

Directions: Saw off end studs on all four mini pegs. For shorter Santas, shorten pegs as desired. Drill a 1/16-inch hole in cut end of each peg, centering the holes.

With pliers, pry open four eye screws just enough to be able to slip them around eyes of remaining screws. Fasten opened screws to pegs in predrilled holes.

Paint the upper two-thirds of chunky pegs with Fire Red or Christmas Green and lower one-third with Black for boots. Paint upper three-fourths of thinner pegs with Fire Red or Christmas Green and lower one-fourth with the opposite color (Christmas Green or Fire Red) for mittens. Set pegs aside to dry.

Sand and seal surface of egg. Paint entire egg either Fire Red or Christmas Green. When dry, mentally divide the egg in half—upper, narrower half will be Santa's face and lower, wider half will be Santa's body. With pencil, draw in belt around egg at halfway point. Using Fig. 1 and photo as a guide, use pencil to draw face on egg freehand, overlapping belt in front with beard.

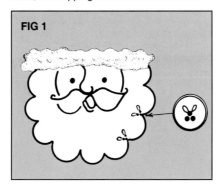

FIG 1

Basecoat face with Flesh. Paint beard and mustache with gesso. Paint belt Black. Use a small flat brush to float Coral over top edge of mustache and around nose for a rosy face. Referring to photo, use a fine liner to draw a scalloped outline around beard with watered-down Salem Green. In same way, outline mustache, adding a few fine lines to resemble hair. If desired, add curls to beards.

For holly on beards, use Christmas Green to paint folk art pollywogs inside points of scalloped outline. Next, dip tip of fine brush handle in Fire Red and dab on egg between leaves for berries, redipping handle in paint for each new berry. Use same technique to paint Black eyes right above Santa's cheeks.

Using just a hint of Fire Red, float a rosy highlight on the end of Santa's nose and overstroke his Coral cheeks.

For textured fur trim, let some gesso dry out just enough to be slightly stiff and tacky. Use an old brush to apply tacky gesso at tip of hat and around its rim. Also apply tacky gesso around top of boots and mittens (see photo). Allow extra time for drying. When dry, apply a second coat, if necessary, for a fluffy dimensional appearance.

Add stripes, hearts or holly to Santa's suit as desired. Personalize and date ornament on back. Let dry before varnishing painted pieces. Let varnish dry completely.

Referring to photo, mark screw positions on Santa's body. Carefully drill small hole in body at each mark and attach four eye screws. Slip on opened eye screws, attaching arms and legs, and gently close eyes with pliers. To make Santa sit, place the leg eye screws more to the front of body. Sit Santa in an egg cup or on a wooden curtain ring.

To hang Santa, drill final hole at top of wood egg and attach eye screw. Thread ribbon through eye screw and tie a bow.✳

HAVE A BEARY CHRISTMAS!

BOTH children and adults can have fun making dough ornaments—whether it's the merry little bears above or the scentsational cinnamon bears at right!

HO-HO-DOUGH BEARS

Materials needed (Makes 2 dozen bears): Pattern; for dough recipe—2 cups flour, 1/2 cup salt, 1 teaspoon dry mustard and 1/2 to 3/4 cup water; thin wire; cookie sheet; vegetable cooking spray; acrylic paints—brown, cream, black, red, white, Kelly green and metallic gold; artist's brushes—No. 00 and No. 1 liner brushes; gloss varnish.

Directions: Preheat oven to 300°. Very lightly coat cookie sheet with vegetable cooking spray. Mix flour with salt and dry

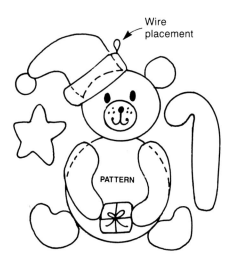

Wire placement

PATTERN

mustard. Add enough water to make a stiff dough. Knead dough for 5 minutes. Dough should be smooth, but pliable. If necessary, add drops of water to dough while kneading.

To prevent dough from drying out, place it in a plastic bag. Break off a small piece and start shaping bear directly on prepared cookie sheet. Start with flattened ball for body. Use pattern as a guide to determine correct size.

Use pattern as guide to shape two legs. Lightly smooth a drop of water in each spot where legs will be attached. Position legs according to pattern.

Form either a candy cane, a Christmas package or a star. Form two arms. For candy cane, use a drop of water to attach an arm to left-hand side of bear first. Next, attach candy cane to bear so hooked end overlaps the arm. Finally, attach second arm to right-hand side of bear so paw overlaps bottom of candy cane. The package and star are attached to body of bear first. The two arms are then attached to look as though bear is holding either the package or star. Always use a drop of water to attach pieces.

Make another flattened circle for bear's head. See pattern for size. Use a drop of water to add a very small flat circle to head for muzzle. Add a tiny ball to muzzle for nose.

Shape hat and attach with a drop of water to one side of bear's head. Make long, flat piece for hatband. Add ball to end of hat and a flattened ball next to hat for ear.

To make hanger, cut a 1-inch piece of wire. Fold wire in half and twist the ends together. Insert wire into hat. See pattern for placement. Bake dough bears for about 2 hours or until bears are completely hard. Let cool.

Paint bears brown. Paint inner ear, muzzle and bottoms of feet with cream color. Paint Santa's hat red with white hatband and white pom-pom. Paint star metallic gold, package green with red ribbon and candy cane white, adding red stripes when dry. Paint facial features in black.

When paint is dry, dip each bear in varnish. Hang bears to dry. Let varnish dry thoroughly before dipping in varnish again. Coat each bear twice.✳

CINNAMON BEARS

Materials needed: Bear-shaped cookie cutter (or shape of your choice); for cinnamon dough recipe—1 cup cinnamon; 4 tablespoons white glue; 3/4 cup water; thin drinking straw; waxed paper; sandpaper; acrylic paints in colors of your choice; assorted small artist's brushes; 1/2 yard of 1/8- or 1/16-inch-wide ribbon for each ornament; standard painting supplies.

Note: These aromatic bears are *not* edible, so keep them out of the reach of children.

Directions: Mix cinnamon, glue and water together. Refrigerate for 2 hours. Sprinkle a small amount of additional cinnamon on work surface. Knead dough until smooth. Roll to 1/4 inch thick. Cut shapes. Use straw to poke a hole through top of each shape for hanging. Set forms on waxed paper and let air-dry for 4 days, turning twice a day. Sand any rough edges. Paint and decorate as desired. Attach ribbon for hanging.✳

PRECIOUS MEMORIES

BY R. GOUBEAUX, WEST HOLLYWOOD, CALIFORNIA

Glass Christmas tree ornaments make a distinctive sound when they are dropped and broken— a muffled *pop* and then a tinkle of paper-thin fragments.

Even though my view is blocked by the tree as I hear that sound, I know instinctively which ornament it is. And my daughter Debbie's yelp only confirms my worst fears.

She's kneeling by a tiny mound of sparkling shards as I approach. "It —it slipped," she moans, her eyes filling with sadness.

Staring at the remains of my most precious Christmas memory, I'm filled with a wave of unreasonable grief and anger. "Go and get the vacuum," I order bluntly. Tears flow freely down her cheeks as Debbie slinks from the room.

Carefully picking up one of the fragments, I fight back tears of my own. Closing my eyes, I can picture the magnificent ornament—a delicate blue-and gold "balloon" with a small glass gondola suspended by golden threads. Riding in the gondola is a tiny figure of Santa Claus.

As a girl, I could sit for hours by my grandma's Christmas tree watching that ornament as it turned and twinkled. The balloon was very special to Grandma—it was one of the few possessions that somehow survived her arduous immigration from Germany and many hard years building a farm in Ohio. More recently, it and another ornament—a glass bear—had been the only remainders of her I could actually still touch.

"The teddy bear!" I gasp, surprising myself. Suddenly I feel an overwhelming need to hold that ornament —to assure myself that it is still intact.

Debbie comes dragging the vacuum into the room, but stops short at the sight of me rummaging almost recklessly through the boxes of ornaments.

Then I find it—that blue glass teddy bear with a small red heart painted on its chest. Cradling the ornament in my cupped hands fills me with a warm feeling of well-being.

What powerful emotions these bits of glass and glitter hold! The little bear brings forth a rush of memories— Grandma in her special Christmas apron..."snickerdoodles" warm from her oven...an ancient nativity set on her sideboard...German *Weihnachten* carols sung by the fire...

Debbie sniffs and kneels to pick up the larger pieces of the shattered ornament. I turn away and focus on the tree. There are other ornaments...other memories.

A hand-carved wooden snowman reminds me of a girlhood Christmas trip with Mom and Dad.

From a bottom branch hangs a miniature metal tractor, too heavy for the top of the tree. It was a gift from the implement dealer when Bill and I bought an old John Deere—our first "big" purchase as newlyweds.

Nearby there is a pale-blue plaster Madonna and child ornament. Imprinted on the back is the Bible verse "Mary treasured all these things and reflected on them in her heart..." It was my mother's favorite ornament.

The vacuum cleaner roars to life, startling me out of my reverie. Watching Debbie sweep up the shreds of glass, though, just brings another memory—one that hasn't come in years.

I can see myself as a girl in Grandma's house once more...but this time the scene is clouded with pain. I'm balanced on a chair, admiring her lovely porcelain Nativity set, when accidentally I knock one of the Three Wise Men from the sideboard. It explodes into pieces on the hardwood floor.

Grandma comes rushing in, and—sure that I'll be punished—I begin to cry inconsolably.

Grandma grabs me up into her arms. "Are you all right, child?"

"Uh-huh," I choke out through my tears. "I'm sorry that I broke your wise man."

She gives me a hug. "That doesn't matter, dear. It was only a *thing*, and people are much more important than things."

Sitting down with me in her lap, Grandma adjusts her glasses and stares for a moment off into the distance. "Do you know what else is more important than things?" she asks after a moment.

"No," I reply.

"Memories," Grandma says wistfully. "Things get broken or lost, and people pass away. But as long as you remember someone in your heart, they'll live forever. Memories are most important of all..."

All at once, I'm back in my own living room— seeing for the first time the hurt my daughter feels.

"Honey," I murmur. "did I ever tell you about Great-Grandma's Nativity?"

Debbie doesn't look at me. I reach out to embrace her...and the blue glass bear slides from my hand, then hits the floor with a *pop*.

"Oh, Mom!" Debbie wails. "Not your bear, too!"

I hug her tightly. "It slipped," I say matter-of-factly. "Guess you're not the only butterfingers in the family."

"But Mom...that was all you had left of Great-Grandma's."

"That's not true," I say, looking my daughter in the eyes. "I still have all my memories. And Debbie, *those* are most important of all."

They Wish You
A MERRY CHRISTMAS!

Built way back in 1817, Irma and Lloyd Esbenshade's Manheim, Pennsylvania farmhouse has seen almost two centuries of Christmases. With the help of this dairy couple, the season is sure to be celebrated there for many years to come.

That's because the Esbenshades believe in decking the halls and radiating holiday cheer from every inch of their historic brick home.

"Dressing up the house for Christmas makes me so happy!" Irma grins. "With Lloyd's help, I put together our decorations myself. And I use natural materials for a true country feel."

Irma's feelings for country are demonstrated most dramatically by the evergreen welcoming wreaths in every window—all *20* of them! A friendly candle flickers on each sill. Out front, an antique sleigh—filled with gifts and a fresh-cut Christmas tree —adds to the season's greetings she delights in supplying.

> *"I tuck baskets of greens and gifts into every nook and cranny."*

Inside, an old-fashioned Colonial fireplace crackles its own warm welcome…an assignment, despite appearances, at which it's still relatively new!

"I'd dreamed of having a fireplace like that ever since I saw one pictured on a Christmas card," Irma relates. "So we built it ourselves—as a Bicentennial project in 1976! In keeping with our country decor, the mantel was cut from a support beam salvaged from an old barn.

"I tuck baskets of greens, pinecones, bright bows, poinsettias and gaily wrapped gifts into every nook and cranny besides!" admits Irma, who also opens the farmhouse to bed-and-breakfast guests. And among those and her other holiday accents, there's another special country one. She's taken an old metal-pronged corn dryer…and transformed it into a strikingly different Christmas tree.

But, as Irma observes, decorating for the season can actually be one good way to enhance its true meaning. So there's one other special "touch" she and Lloyd insist on. On an antique sausage-making bench behind the sofa, the Esbenshades prominently display a family Bible —then keep it opened all season to the inspiring scene of the Nativity!

CHRISTMAS TAKES A BOUGH in beautiful fashion at farmhouse of Irma (far left) and Lloyd (left) Esbenshade. At bottom of opposite page, sleigh (inspected by curious cat) puts country stamp on season …and wreaths in every window extend welcome! Below, interesting old marble roller (made by hand by Irma's father) and cob-decked corn dryer tree blend right in—while Bible gets prominent place near garland-clad Bicentennial fireplace (below left).

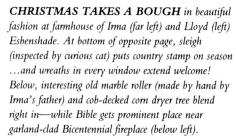

MEMORIES ARE GOLDEN

BY BARBARA CAPELLE
NEW CANAAN, CONNECTICUT

IT WON'T be long now! In only weeks, there will be cut-glass bowls on our dining room table brimming with spruce cones painted gold.

Golden, too, are my memories of growing up in Connecticut in the 1930's. Back then, I didn't need a calendar to conclude Christmas was close. All it took was my father's announcement we were heading out to hunt for ground pine.

It didn't disturb me that "the woods" to which we were trekking were but a 2-minute walk away—just beyond the stone wall across the road. I had been anticipating our father-daughter adventure for days already!

We'd gather those graceful "club moss" vines, rolling them into skeins and popping them into the burlap bag. Then, home again, my mother and I would tie the sections of vine with green cord to form long, lacy roping.

One year, we draped our creations along the front porch railing, catching the loops onto the pillars with perky bows Mom had cut from red flowered percale; another time, we wound our Merry Christmas message around the mailbox post.

No matter where our ground pine ended up, however, we always finished with a spray of evergreens for the front door. That, Dad insisted, was even more tasteful than the traditionally round wreath. (Looking back, I suspect he preferred the spray because it was easier to assemble!)

Our tree itself never appeared until Christmas Eve—but there were always other indicators of the season.

The old oak sideboard was whisked clear to make room for a green ceramic sleigh. The sleigh soon would be heaped with shiny ornaments that—reflected in the sideboard's mirror—added a double touch of cheer to our dining room.

And it seems each year there'd be a special harbinger of the holidays. One year, Mom and I clipped a few dozen cones from the big spruce outside my bedroom window.

"They're *ugly*," I thought, frowning at the closed and frozen seed cases. "They'll spoil our tree!"

"Wait till tomorrow," my mother suggested with a smile, setting the cones on the kitchen radiator.

What an awakening I had the next morning! Thoroughly thawed, the cones had popped open overnight, spewing feathery seeds all over the newspaper spread beneath them.

That afternoon we gilded the cones, dabbing them with tiny brushes dipped in a mixture of gold powder and oil. Afterward, Dad topped the cones with eyelet screws, and we threaded them with thin red ribbon. Then, for the next week or so, they went on display in cut-glass bowls on the dining room table.

These days, once-enticing ground pine has become a protected plant in our state. So I gather it now only in recollections of my girlhood. But that's sufficient.

So much of the magic of this season, I've learned, lies in anticipation—whether of Christmas present *or* Christmas past!

CHRISTMAS IS...

Christmastime is green 'n' red 'n'
Candy canes 'n' gingerbread 'n'
Carols sung with voices joyful,
Stockings hung, all stuffed and toyful...
Twine and tape and lists and labels,
Cards addressed at kitchen tables

Christmastime is faces glowing,
Sidewalk Santas ho-ho-ho-ing...
Streets and stores all thickly peopled,
Music chimed from churches steepled.
Plays and pageants, lines forgotten—
Bright foil wings and beards of cotton.

Christmastime is wrapped in wonder:
Piles of presents stacked up under
Christmas trees, so green and piny,
Dressed their best in tinsel shiny...
Mistletoe and stolen kisses,
Flakes of snow and Kringled Krisses.

Christmastime is goodies baking
And the sight of children making
Glue-'n'-paper decorations,
Filling holiday vacations
With their smiles and with their laughter,
And with memories kept long after...

Christmastime is scenes of mangers,
Kindnesses to friends and strangers...
Porch lights on and candles burning,
Loved ones, far from home, returning.
Christmastime is meant for sharing—
People loving, people caring.

By Diane Siebert
Crooked River Ranch, Oregon

DOOR DECOR ADDS JOY!

FRIENDS and visitors will feel welcome when they see this ruffled wreath on your door. Using bleached muslin and a stenciled motif around the border, it beautifully captures the season's joyous spirit.

STENCILED RUFFLED WREATH

Materials needed: Stencil pattern; 2 yards of bleached muslin; 1/4 yard of 45-inch scarlet red muslin; matching threads; acrylic craft or fabric paints—red, green and brown; two No. 2 and two No. 8 stencil brushes; container of water; plastic lid to use as palette; paper towels; 12- x 16-inch piece of stencil acetate; fine-line permanent-ink marker; stencil knife or craft knife with sharp No. 11 blade; masking tape; 12-inch Styrofoam wreath; tacky craft glue; small saw; large safety pin; iron; standard sewing supplies.

Finished size: Wreath is about 18 inches in diameter.

Directions: Wash fabrics to remove sizing. Press to dry. Cut one 15- x 72-inch strip of bleached muslin for wreath and one 6- x 45-inch strip of red muslin for bow.

Place acetate over stencil pattern and trace design with permanent-ink marker, tracing placement line as well. Place acetate on a thick layer of newspaper to protect work surface. Holding craft knife like a pencil, begin at top of each shape and slowly pull knife until each shape is completely cut. Repair cutting mistakes by applying tape to both sides of acetate and recutting.

Fold bleached muslin strip in half lengthwise and press a crease down entire length of fabric. This is outer edge of ruffle and will be used for placement of stencil. Open fabric and tape, right side up, to flat surface. Tape stencil to left-hand end of fabric, matching placement line to crease line. Use No. 2 brushes to stencil brown and green trees. Always use a clean, dry brush for each new color. Use No. 8 brush for red letters.

To stencil, place a small amount of paint on palette. Dip tip of brush in paint and remove excess by wiping brush on a folded paper towel. (Too much paint can seep under stencil edges, ruining the design.) Hold brush perpendicular to stencil, and dab brush in an up and down motion over cutout areas of stencil. Working in a circular motion from the outer edge of stencil, build up color by continuing to dab brush on fabric. Do not build up color by adding more paint to brush.

When first motif is complete, carefully remove stencil and wipe it clean. Reposition stencil so left-hand tree overlaps the right-hand tree just stenciled and stencil a second motif. Continue to repeat the motif in this manner across the length of fabric.

Clean brushes with soap and water. Allow paint to dry 24 hours. Heat-set colors by ironing for 25 to 30 seconds with a dry iron set at a low cotton setting.

Wreath assembly: Hem each short end of fabric by turning raw edges under 1/4 inch twice and stitching near edge. Fold fabric in half lengthwise, right sides together, and stitch a 1/4-inch seam along length of fabric. Turn piece right side out. Press.

On right side of fabric, stitch across its length 1 inch from seamline. This will form interior ruffle when put on foam wreath.

For casing, measure width of foam wreath and add 1/4 inch to this measurement. The total should be about 3-1/8 inches. Stitch across length of fabric this far from last row of stitching. This stitching should be between the last row of stitching and foldline. Use saw to slit wreath on an angle. Carefully slip the stitched covering on wreath. Glue slit on wreath closed. Tape around slit until glue sets. Adjust gathers to cover slit. Attach large safety pin to top of wreath for hanging.

Bow: Fold red muslin strip in half lengthwise, right sides together. Stitch a 1/4-inch seam across all three raw edges, leaving an opening in center for turning. Turn piece right side out. Press. Turn in raw edges and hand-stitch opening closed. Tie a bow. Pin or stitch bow to wreath, covering point where ends of ruffle meet.✳

Placement line

RUFFLED WREATH STENCIL

HUNG BY THE CHIMNEY WITH CARE

CHRISTMAS DECORATING and cherished traditions go hand in hand—especially when you let handmade crafts like this crocheted stocking show off the spirit of the season!

CROCHETED CHRISTMAS STOCKING

Materials needed: Any 4-ply worsted-weight acrylic yarn—1 ball natural, 1 ball deep green, 1 ball cranberry; size G crochet hook (or size needed for correct gauge); yarn needle; safety pin; 1/3 yard of 36-inch-wide cotton fabric in coordinating color; matching thread; standard sewing supplies.

Gauge: 14 sts = 4 inches and 12 rows = 4 inches when worked in seed stitch pattern.

Stitches used:
Bobbles: Work 1 dc; * yo, insert hook between dc just made and previous st, yo, draw loop to front; rep from * three more times so there are nine loops on hook; yo and draw yarn through all nine loops; ch 2.

Seed Stitch: Rnd 1: * Work 1 dc in next st, 1 sc in next st; repeat from * around. Rnd 2

and all other rnds: * Work 1 sc in each dc and 1 dc in each sc around.

Corded rib: This rnd is worked in sc from left to right, causing stitches to twist and create a decorative effect. Work as follows: Insert hook into front loop of first stitch to the right; pull yarn through, twisting hook to face downward at the same time—this movement will pull yarn through fabric, but not through loop already on hook; yo and draw through to finish off sc as usual.

Directions: Stocking is worked from top down. Mark last st of first rnd with a safety pin. Work to marked st; remove pin; work next st; reinsert pin, marking last st of new rnd. This is center back of stocking.

With natural, ch 45 and sl st in first ch to form a ring.

Rnds 1-8: Ch 1; work even in seed st over next 44 sts. (End each rnd with a sl st in sl st of previous rnd.) Repeat this rnd for a total of eight rnds.
Rnd 9: Ch 1; work 1 sc in each st around. Drop natural.
Rnd 10: With green, ch 1, * work 1 bobble in next st, 1 sc in next st; repeat from * around. Fasten off green.

Rnd 11: Pick up natural, ch 1, * work 1 sc in each of 2 ch at top of bobble, skip next sc and repeat from * around. Drop natural.
Rnds 12-13: Repeat rnds 10 and 11 once with red and natural.
Rnds 14-15: Repeat rnds 10 and 11 once with green and natural.
Rnds 16-17: Ch 1, * work 1 sc in each of next 2 sts with natural; 1 sc in each of next 2 sts with green; rep from * around. Drop green.
Rnds 18-19: Ch 1, * work 1 sc in each of next 2 sts with red; 1 sc in each of next 2 sts with natural; rep from * around. Drop red.
Rnds 20-21: Repeat rnds 16 and 17.
Rnd 22: Pick up natural, ch 1, sc in each sc around. Drop natural.
Rnd 23: With red, ch 1, work corded rib around. Fasten off red.
Rnd 24: Pick up natural, ch 1, work 1 sc in back of loop of each st in last natural color rnd.
Rnds 25-26: With natural, repeat last 2 rnds.
Rnds 27-34: With green, work even in seed st pattern for 8 rnds.

Heel: Heel is worked in seed st pattern with green, short-rowing for 9 rows as follows.
Heel row 1: From center back, work in pattern for 13 sts; sk 1, sc in next st; turn.
Heel row 2: Skip 1 and work in pattern for 13 sts; skip sl st from previous row and work in pattern for 13 sts; skip 1, sc in next st; turn.
Heel row 3: Skip 1 and work in pattern for 24 sts; skip 1 and sc in next st; turn.
Heel rows 4-8: Repeat last row, working 2 sts less in each pattern section, in each row.
Heel row 9: Skip 1 and work in pattern for 6 sts, ending at center back. Do not turn work.
Last heel rnd: In seed st, work 6 sts; pick up and work 6 sts along heel shaping; work last 6 sts; sl st to first st.

Foot: Working over 36 sts, repeat the patterned calf section in reverse order—corded rib; checkerboard; bobbles. End this section with a natural sc round.

Toe: With red, work * 1 rnd in seed st; 1 rnd in sc, decreasing 3 sts evenly spaced; repeat from * five times until 21 sts are left; sl st to first st.

Cut yarn, leaving a 12-inch end. Using yarn needle, weave 12-inch end through remaining 21 sts. Pull yarn tight to gather toe. Secure and weave-in all loose ends.

Loop: With double strand of natural, ch 16; sl st in first ch to form a ring. Cut yarn, leaving a 6-inch end. Pull yarn through last st to secure. With yarn needle, sew loop to stocking about 1 inch down from top edge at center back. Secure and weave in ends.

Lining: Fold lining fabric in half, right sides together. Place crocheted stocking on fabric and trace around its shape. Add 1/4-inch seam allowance and cut out. Sew pieces together on tracing line, leaving top open. Clip seam allowance at curves. Do not turn fabric stocking right side out.

Insert fabric stocking into crocheted stocking. Turn raw fabric edge under to second round from the top. Use matching color thread and a small overcast stitch to sew lining to stocking at turned edge.✳

A PRETTY PASTA ANGEL

THESE ornaments are a dandy do-ahead project for gifts, bazaar items and for your family's own tree, too.

PASTA ANGEL

Materials needed: 4 smaller-size elbow macaroni; 2 medium-size elbow macaroni; 1 rigatoni noodle, about 1-1/4 inches long; tiny macaroni rings; 1 bowtie macaroni; 1 wooden bead, about 3/4 inch in diameter (can be macrame bead); any fast-drying craft glue; scrap board with nail; can of quick-drying white enamel spray paint; permanent-ink, fine-tipped felt-tip pens—black and red; small gold star; gold Christmas string or colored yarn.

Directions: Glue two smaller-size elbow macaroni to one end of rigatoni noodle (each noodle making a half circle) to form the neck of the angel. Let dry. Glue two smaller-size elbow macaroni to other end of rigatoni noodle to form the base of the angel. Let dry.

Glue the wooden bead onto neck for head; let dry. (If you are using a macrame bead with a hole in it, fill in the hole with cotton. This makes next step easier.) Glue several layers of macaroni rings onto head to form hair—give the hair more depth by adding more layers of rings.

Form angel's arms by gluing two medium-size elbow macaroni to front of rigatoni noodle, one on either side. To form wings, center bowtie macaroni on back of rigatoni noodle, glue in place and let dry.

To make it easier to paint and dry angel, hammer a nail into a piece of scrap wood and stand angel up on it. This also makes it easier to "mass-produce" angels.

Spray-paint using quick-drying white enamel paint. Let dry. Next, use black marker to draw angel's eyes and nose and red marker to make mouth (see photo). For an added touch, glue a small gold star (or small sprig of holly or miniature candle) to angel's hands.

Tie Christmas string or colored yarn around angel's neck and hang.✳

FIT FOR A FESTIVE FEAST

YOU CAN brighten your holiday table with this handsome set of homemade place mats, napkins and ties. Each item's easy and inexpensive to make, especially if you use scraps of materials.

RAG-ART HOLIDAY PLACE SETTING

Materials needed (for one place mat, one napkin and one tie): Chart; 13-1/2-inch x 20-3/4-inch piece of needlepoint canvas, 3.3 holes per inch; plastic Ragpoint needle; cotton or polyester/cotton fabric in these amounts—1-1/4 yards muslin, 3/4 yard plus one 16-1/2-inch square green fabric, and 1/4 yard plus one 16-1/2-inch square red fabric; 1-1/2-inch wooden heart; 7/8-inch wooden heart; red and green acrylic paint; paintbrush; glue; standard sewing supplies.

Directions:
PLACE MAT: Preshrink fabric. Cut or tear fabric into 1-inch strips in crosswise direction (from selvage to selvage).

Prepare needlepoint canvas by turning and pressing back three holes along all four edges.

Thread needle with one strip of green fabric. Do not knot! All fabric tails should be caught in stitches on back side of place mat. Starting in the center of one long outer edge, stitch through both layers of canvas, whipstitching to cover outer canvas thread. Continue around entire place mat in green.

Locate center point of canvas and center point of pattern. Begin at this point to stitch design on canvas using a half cross-stitch. (See Fig. 1.) Be careful not to pull stitches too tight.

Stitch heart in red, tree in green and tree trunk in brown, following chart for color placement of stitches. Stitch background of place mat in muslin.

Finish the border by stitching one round of red and one of green. (The final border row is the already completed whipstitched edge.)

After stitching is completed, square place mat by pulling on opposite corners as much as needed. Pin place mat to ironing board or carpet. Apply dampened press cloth and steam-press to set shape. Let dry.

NAPKIN: Place squares of green and red fabrics with right sides together. Stitch 1/4-inch seam all around, leaving 2-inch opening for turning. Turn right side out and press. Stitch opening closed.

NAPKIN TIE: Paint wooden hearts red. Let dry. Glue small heart on top of large heart. Let dry. Tear a 1-inch x 23-3/4-inch strip of green fabric. Wrap around napkin and tie into bow. To complete tie, remove napkin and glue small wooden hearts to center of bow.✳

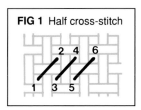

FIG 1 Half cross-stitch

COLOR KEY
⊟ Brown
◢ Red
♥ Green
☐ Muslin

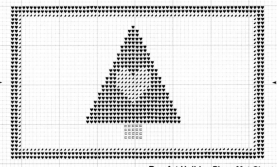

▲ **Rag Art Holiday Place Mat Chart**

SEW A SAINT NICK!

YOU BETTER watch out—making and displaying this old-fashioned Father Christmas doll is apt to bring some merry memories of past holidays to mind. With his sack and backpack filled with goodies, Santa's presence on a mantel or table will remind visitors of the spirit of giving at Christmastime.

FATHER CHRISTMAS DOLL

Materials needed: Patterns on pages 83 and 84; freezer paper; pencil; hot glue gun; 1-inch sponge brush; water-base varnish; paper towels; one adult-size cloth or leather glove; 9-inch gold color chain, matching jump rings, several small gold color bells; standard sewing and painting supplies.

FOR DOLL BODY: 1/4 yard Osnaburg fabric (muslin can be substituted); matching regular and heavy-duty threads; soft-sculpture or doll needle; unspun wool for hair and beard (unbraided Curly Crepe Wool Doll Hair will work); polyester stuffing; 6- x 4-inch piece of

quilt batting; ultra-fine permanent-ink markers such as Pilot pen SC-UF or Pigma 01 SDK in brown and black; fabric paints—white, black, flesh, dark brown, gray-blue, barn red and yellow for facial features; artist's brushes—No. 1 liner and No. 2 flat.

FOR ROBE: 1/4 yard red wool or felt; 1/8 yard or scraps of real or synthetic fur; matching regular and heavy-duty threads; large pearl, button or bell for point of hood.

FOR GOWN (optional): 1/4 yard fabric of your choice (doll shown is dressed in a royal-looking paisley print); 30 inches of 5/8- or 3/4-inch gold metallic trim; matching threads.

FOR SACK AND BACKPACK: 12- x 6-inch piece of loosely woven wool fabric or burlap; matching thread; 1/2 yard of gold cord; a variety of Christmas greenery, pinecones, pine branches and dried flowers; a variety of miniature toys; leather scraps (can be cut from an old wallet, purse or large glove).

FOR STAND: 8- x 5-1/2- x 1/2-inch wood board; 9-inch piece of 1/4-inch doweling; drill with 1/4-inch bit.

Finished size: Santa stands 12-1/2 inches high, including stand.

Directions:
Body: Trace patterns to freezer paper and cut out. Place body pattern, shiny side down, on wrong side of Osnaburg fabric. Press pattern with warm (not hot) iron, temporarily adhering it to fabric. Fold fabric in half and pin right sides together. Set a very short stitch length on machine. Sew around pattern, leaving an opening at side for turning and back-stitching at beginning and end of seam. Cut out doll, leaving a very narrow seam allowance. Remove pattern. Clip curves and turn doll right side out.

Firmly stuff legs and hands. (Stuffing can be pushed in place with a long, thin stick or knitting needle.) Topstitch across elbows (see the pattern). Lightly stuff upper arms. Topstitch across shoulders as marked. Finish stuffing head and body. Turn in raw edges and hand-sew opening closed.

Nose: Thread doll needle with a double strand of heavy-duty thread. Bring needle through back of doll's head, coming out at dot No. 1 (see pattern). Reinsert needle very close to same dot, go under stuffing and exit at dot No. 2. Reinsert needle close to same dot and exit at dot No. 3. Continue in this manner until you've reached dot No. 6. Exit at back of head. Knot and cut thread.

Face: Use sponge brush to paint front of head flesh. Let dry. Dip flat brush in dark brown paint, blotting on paper towel until brush is almost dry. Lightly scrub brush on doll's face in eye area to transfer a light shade of brown (see Fig. 1). This technique is called dry-brushing. If more intense color is desired, add additional layers. Dry-brush dark brown down one side of nose. See Fig. 1.

With pencil, draw in an iris on each side of nose. See Fig. 2. With liner brush, paint pencil lines gray-blue.

Add a dab of yellow to white. Dry-brush under eyes and tops of cheeks (see Fig. 3).

With liner brush, paint corners of eyes white. Paint pupils black as shown in Fig. 4.

Paint tiny white highlights in eyes at 2 and 7 o'clock positions. With flat brush, dry-brush red on cheeks and forehead as shown in Fig. 5.

With black pen, outline top of eyes and outside corners as shown in Fig. 6.

With brown pen, draw small lines around eyes as shown in Fig. 7 and a few squiggly lines on forehead for wrinkles.

When dry, sponge-brush a thin coat of water-base varnish on face. Let dry.

Stand: Purchase or cut an 8- x 5-1/2- x 1/2-inch wood board, sanding or routing the edges as desired. Drill hole to fit 1/4-inch dowel, positioning it about 3 inches from back and 2 inches from left-hand side. Hot-glue 9-inch dowel in place. Sponge-brush stand with dark brown paint, quickly wiping off wet paint so board is stained brown. When dry, apply water-base varnish.

Dress doll: Secure doll on stand by tying heavy-duty thread several times around doll and dowel. To add girth to Santa's belly, place a 6- x 4-inch piece of batting on front torso. Add stuffing under batting, then tack batting to doll.

Cut two fingers from an adult-size glove.

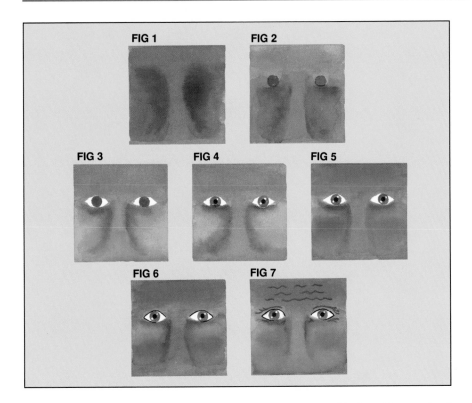

FIG 1 FIG 2

FIG 3 FIG 4 FIG 5

FIG 6 FIG 7

Stitch or glue one to each hand.

To make gown, if desired, cut two 9- x 11-1/4-inch pieces of fabric. Allowing 1/4-inch seams, sew sides, leaving open as marked in Fig. 8. Turn gown right side out, fold under side seams at openings and finger-press. Fold top edge under 1/2 inch and topstitch 1/4 inch from fold for casing. Turn under bottom edge 1/2 inch. Pin or baste gold trim along bottom edge. Topstitch trim in place, sewing hem at same time.

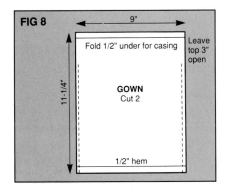

FIG 8

9"

Fold 1/2" under for casing

Leave top 3" open

11-1/4"

GOWN
Cut 2

1/2" hem

Insert heavy-duty thread through casings at neck. Put gown on doll, pulling threads to fit neckline and tie. Loosely wrap remaining gold trim around doll's belly for belt and either hot-glue or hand-stitch in back.

Robe: Use pattern to cut two robes and one hood on fold. Slit one robe piece along fold-line, creating two front pieces. With right sides together, sew shoulder/arm seams, underarm and side seams. Finish edges of front opening and bottom edge with 1/2-inch hems. Turn under neck edge and hand-gather with heavy-duty thread. Put robe on doll and pull gathers to fit, leaving about 1/2 inch gap in front. Tie off thread ends and hot-glue robe in place. Turn cuffs under 1 inch and hand-gather to fit wrists.

Hair: Hot-glue wool for beard from ear level, down under nose and around to other side. Hot-glue wool to top of head, letting loose wool extend down over top of beard. Tie a 3-inch strip of wool in center and hot-glue under nose for mustache. Roll tiny pieces of wool between fingers and hot-glue above eyes for eyebrows.

Hood: With right sides together, sew center back seam. Hem all raw edges 1/4 inch. Turn

right side out. Sew or hot-glue either a large pearl, button or bell to point of hood. Hot-glue hood to Santa's head.

Fur trim: Measure left-hand opening of robe, front of hood and right-hand opening of robe. Cut a 1-inch-wide strip of fur this length. When cutting fur, always cut through backing fabric (or hide) only. Fur scraps can be pieced if necessary. Hot-glue fur in place. Start at bottom of one side of robe, continue around outer edge of hood and go down opposite side of robe, ending at bottom. Hot-glue doll's feet to stand. If gown was omitted, hand-stitch robe closed.

Backpack: Cut a 10- x 3-inch strip of leather. Glue 3-inch ends together in back, overlapping 1/4 to 1/2 inch. Glue bottom edges together, creating a pouch.

Cut a 1/4-inch-wide leather strip long enough to loosely go around doll's neck. Hot-glue strap to one side of backpack, bring around doll's neck, under Santa's beard, and hot-glue to other side of backpack.

Hot-glue Christmas greenery in pack. Add dried flowers, berries, pinecones or small ornaments. Hot-glue pack to Santa's back.

Bells: Using jump rings, attach several bells to each end of 9-inch chain. Put over one of doll's hands, tacking chain to glove or robe. Hot-glue a small toy under same arm.

Santa sack: Cut a 12- x 6-inch wool or burlap rectangle. With right sides facing, fold rectangle so 6-inch edges meet. Sew side and bottom edges, leaving 1/4-inch seams. Turn sack right side out and fill with crumpled newspaper, leaving top 2 inches unstuffed. Tie gold cord around top. Hot-glue pinecones and small Christmas decorations to cord. Hot-glue sack to stand with several small toys in front.✳

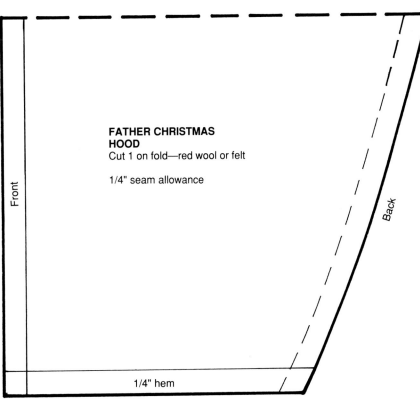

Front

FATHER CHRISTMAS HOOD
Cut 1 on fold—red wool or felt

1/4" seam allowance

Back

1/4" hem

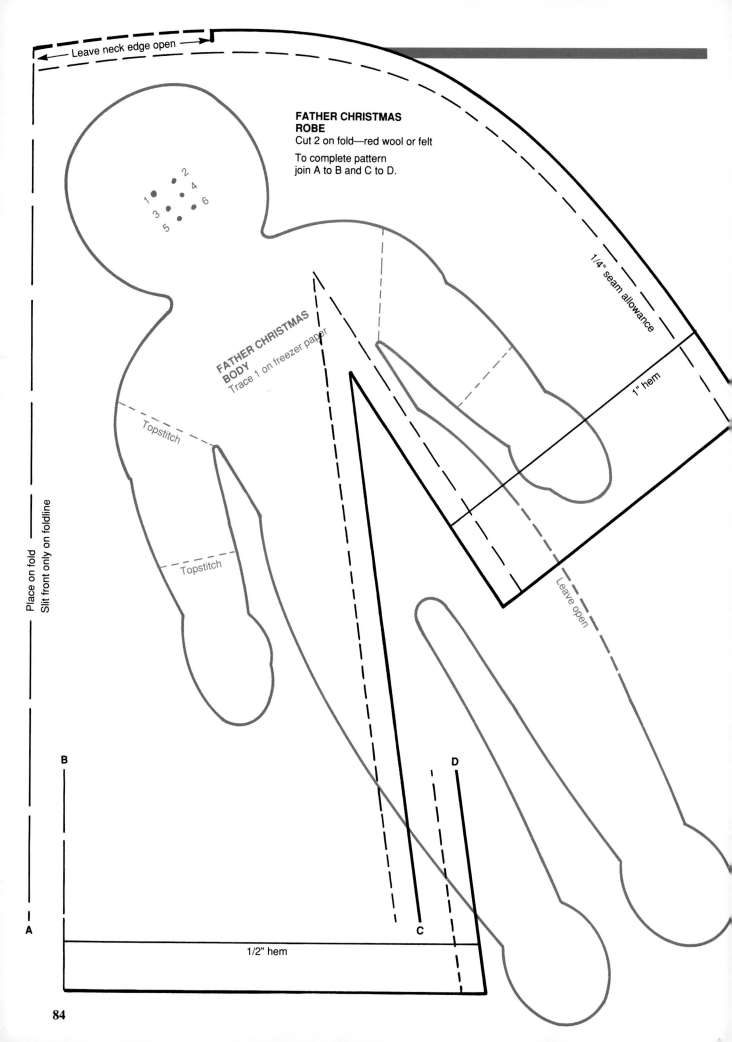

Leave neck edge open

**FATHER CHRISTMAS
ROBE**
Cut 2 on fold—red wool or felt

To complete pattern
join A to B and C to D.

1
2
4
3
6
5

1/4" seam allowance

1" hem

FATHER CHRISTMAS
BODY
Trace 1 on freezer paper

Topstitch

Topstitch

Leave open

Place on fold
Slit front only on foldline

B

D

A

C

1/2" hem

Bethany Has a
SOFT TOUCH FOR SANTA

BY DIANNE L. BEETLER, ALTONA, ILLINOIS

Ask Osco, Illinois hog farmer's wife Bethany Lowe why Santa's such a popular person, and she'll likely answer, "Because he's a *country* boy".

How does Bethany know? Simple. For many people coast to coast, she's the one who's made the old-fashioned fellow what he is today!

"I'd always been enchanted by the antique Santas modeled after St. Nicholas himself," she explains. "But items like that are too expensive for most of us. So I decided to try my crafting hand at designing a few modern-day versions."

Soon, this energetic mother of four found her on-farm sideline—aptly named "Nostalgia for Nicholas"—absolutely snowballing!

"There are so many sides to Santa's well-rounded personality," she smiles, "that when I start dreaming up characters…well, the sky's the limit. In all, I now have 28 soft-sculpture designs—each unique.

"For instance, I outfit my 'Mountain Delivery Santa' with miniature snowshoes, and 'Prairie Santa' wears real buckskin breeches. My 'Southwestern Santa', meanwhile, is draped with a woven fringed blanket patterned after an Indian tapestry."

There's an abundance of authentic country elsewhere besides in Bethany's Santas. "The curly wool for their whiskers comes from an Iowa farmer's sheep," she points out. "And local families piece the costumes I design from recycled fabrics and furs."

The farm family that's closest to Bethany's Santas, though, is her own brood!

"We work together in a sunny corner of my husband Curt's machine shed," she details. "Son Heath, 20, stuffs the papier-mache bodies, and 9-year-old Erin attaches the leather boots she stitches. Next, Chad, 19, Nathan, 12, and their father fashion wooden stands and accessories while I paint expressions on the canvas faces." Taller orders involve a bit more effort, but Bethany's happy to oblige. "Occasionally," she notes, "people will bring me their grandmothers' quilts and ask for an 'Heirloom Santa'. Those 3-foot characters take 3 full days to finish! Still, it's so much fun imagining them spreading cheer…year after year."

For Bethany, lending Curt a hand with their 4,000-head herd is a year-round endeavor, too. Come Christmas, however, it's that right jolly old elf who hogs her attention again!

"I've spent many a Christmas morning—before my family starts stirring—in my workshop, sketching new versions of St. Nick for next year," she admits.

With such early-bird hours, who knows? This year, Bethany might finally meet the famous merry fellow face-to-face!

For more details about Bethany's Santas, write her at R.R. 1, Box 70, Osco IL 61274.

SHE'S SO SMITTEN with St. Nick, Bethany Lowe's workshop resembles the North Pole! Toys are handmade—so is the recycled fur suit!

Their Decorations Echo of Warm
COUNTRY CHRISTMASES

BY NANCY DOHN AND CARLA HOTVEDT, GAINESVILLE, FLORIDA

This couple's holiday decorations make their home inviting by evoking memories of gentler Christmases past.

Decorating for the holidays is a joyous task in most households. In Judy and Direlle Baird's country home, sprucing up for Christmas is a treat they plan for all year long! The Bairds love antiques, folk art and music, and combine all three with special yuletide touches for an old-fashioned country Christmas.

Judy and Direlle love Christmas so much they can hardly wait to start decorating their two-story home near Gainesville, Florida; they usually get started by early autumn!

"We decorate for the holidays at the first opportunity," smiles Direlle, who teaches agriculture engineering at the University of Florida. "We wait just long enough so we don't look like we're rushing things!

"We usually find the first trees available in the area and choose one of the tallest—we seem to choose a larger one every year!—and then try to make it last as long as we can."

Although Florida doesn't get much (if any) snow during the winter, it does get cold enough for the Bairds to use their fireplace, and the warm glow that emanates from their home during the holidays is always a welcome sight for visitors.

As soon as the Bairds greet you in their entryway, you feel as though you've stepped back in time to a gentler, more simple era. A stately grandfather clock stands guard while stuffed bears—nestled in a quilt nearly a century old—gaze up from an antique field cradle the Bairds bought in Pennsylvania.

From deeper inside the house, the scent of clove-studded oranges and spicy potpourri reminds you of Christmases past.

Lush green garlands are swagged with red velvet bows along the banister leading upstairs, and vibrant red poinsettias add bright, festive spots to each room.

"We usually have more than 40 poinsettia plants scattered throughout the house," Judy says with a smile. "Christmas means red and green to me, so we use those colors a lot."

Judy, who co-owns Country Sampler, a local store that specializes in folk art, prefers to use authentic touches in the decorations wherever possible—and that includes the trimmings on the Christmas tree!

The tree, always the focal point of the family room, is never draped in tinsel, but is decorated instead with glass and wooden ornaments and small, subtle strings of lights. "Trimming the tree is my favorite thing," Judy says. "It always brings back all kinds of wonderful memories."

Plaid bows are scattered throughout the branches, and a slightly crooked star makes a sparkling crown.

"We use handmade bows to make the tree look more old-fashioned," Judy explains. "And the star on top is literally falling apart, but we can't bear to part with it. We've had it almost our entire married life."

The tipsy tree-topping star is just one of the holiday traditions that's important to the Bairds. Hanging above the family room's brick fireplace—which is *almost* large enough for Santa himself to slide down!—is a wreath decorated with a French horn and two bugles. Direlle says the instruments reflect his long country heritage, and his musical upbringing, too.

"On my grandfather's farm in Tennessee, music was always an important part of life at any time of year," he says. "It means a lot to me, and Christmas gives us a perfect opportunity to share music and singing with the people in our lives who mean so much to us."

Many friends and relatives have shared the Bairds' love of music in their cozy music room, where Judy plays Christmas songs on the grand piano while Direlle joins in on the trumpet or guitar.

Even when the music room is empty, the Bairds' love of music is obvious. A book of Christmas carols stands ready for use at all times, and figures of Victorian carolers circle a gas lamp atop the piano.

The old-world carolers are just one of the special collections that help countrify the Bairds' "new world" home and add to the old-fashioned feel at the holidays and year-round.

"Collecting hand-hewn oak furniture, old pie safes and other items during vacations has been our favorite hobby for almost 20 years," Judy says.

"Every vacation we go on usually includes browsing for antiques. It began before we were married really. It's sort of a family tradition on my side, from an uncle who was interested in collecting old things."

A cherished cross-stitched sampler on the music

GLOWING LIGHTS *and cheery poinsettias, wreaths and bows welcome guests to the Bairds' home (top); cozy entranceway is perfect spot to share holiday cheer with visitors (left); festive decorations add a touch of elegance to holiday gatherings (above right); Judy and Direlle serenade guests with favorite Christmas carols.*

room wall has seen 144 Christmases! The sampler, which Judy found during a trip to England, was made by a 13-year-old girl named Elizabeth Bainbridge back in 1846.

The Bairds also have collected a number of nutcrackers over the years, and like to display the colorful bunch during the holidays in an old open cupboard.

A large collection of Santa Claus figures, ranging from the size of a thimble to more than 2 ft. tall, adds delightful touches to selected areas throughout the house.

"I've collected Santas for almost 10 years and have some very unusual ones," Judy says.

"One is made of cork and can be used as a bottle stopper. Another is carved on the surface of a wooden sphere, which is cradled on a wheeled base. When you

"We use handmade bows to make the tree look more old-fashioned."

pull a string, the Santa spins round and round!"

Judy has named a few of the figures in her collection, such as the "Old World Santa", named for his rustic appearance. Dressed in red velvet, with hands and face made of burlap, he grasps a clump of twigs over his shoulder instead of a big bundle of toys.

Other Santas have a more traditional look, bending under the burden of bags filled with Christmas delights.

Judy's favorite elf is perched in an antique pie safe in the kitchen, where he can keep a watchful eye on evening meals—served, of course, on bright red plates decorated with festive green Christmas trees!

Judy and Direlle's holiday guests always gravitate to this room and the tempting array of homemade con-

fections, fresh-brewed coffee flavored with vanilla arranged platters of holiday cakes and cookies.

"There's just something special about having friends gather around good food in the kitchen on a winter night," Direlle says.

To enhance that special yuletide glow, the Bairds arrange candles in the middle of a straw wreath surrounded by rustic metal Christmas trees. The candlesticks are old wooden bobbins, shiny from years of spinning in the woolen mills—another instance where past meets present in a gracious home where hospitality and old-time ways are still honored.

"We love to share this time of the year with guests and to bring good cheer and warm feelings to all our friends," Direlle says. "Christmas is a time to relax from our busy schedules and enjoy the fellowship of all the people we love."

Carol's Costumes Help...

SPREAD THE GOOD NEWS

When she gets ready to start stitching a new outfit, farm wife Carol Kremer of Aurora, Nebraska turns to an unusual guide—the greatest story ever told!

"Year's ago," explains the mother of three now-grown daughters, "I was hemming an intricate tunic for our church's Nativity pageant. It suddenly occurred to me how time-consuming such a task must be for mothers who aren't accustomed to sewing."

Before long, Carol's Costumes was born! Carol now custom-crafts Biblical apparel ranging from simple woolen shepherds' frocks and wispy gold-trimmed choir gowns to bejeweled headdresses and robes for the Magi to wear as they follow the star.

"Of course, I don't have photos to show me exactly how soldiers, kings or the Holy Family dressed," she points out. "So I begin with commercial patterns. Then I study illustrations in the Bible—and in Sunday school primers, too—for the finishing touches."

And even when Christmas has passed, her work's not completed.

"With religious dramas becoming more and more popular in worship services, outdoor ministries and vacation Bible schools, I make my costumes washable and durable. Plus, I stitch in plenty of growing room so that they can be used year-round, season after season.

"Actually, it's amazing how this fits in with our grain farming," Carol chuckles. "Usually, I finish up my Easter orders just before my husband, Ron, is ready to start spring planting. Then, after I hop off the combine at the end of harvest, I head directly to my sewing machine to get a jump on the Christmas rush."

"Rush" was the word of the day last Thanksgiving when daughter LeeAnn arrived home from college...and politely requested 23 Christmas pageant costumes for her Sunday school students!

"I was still catching my breath from that when I received an urgent call from a Michigan chaplain in March," Carol recalls. "He needed 13 costumes for a living Last Supper...in time for Palm Sunday!"

No matter how quickly she must make her costumes, however, Carol *always* spares the expense. "I cut them from economical cottons and knits I find at fabric sales. That way, even small country churches can afford them.

"In fact, whenever I get the urge to switch to silks and velvets, I just recall how simple swaddling clothes brought such great joy to our world," Carol quietly offers. "For me, *that's* the true meaning of Christmas."

For information on Carol's costumes, contact her at Rt. 1, Box 105, Aurora NE 68818.

Christmas stars shine in Carol Kremer's design. Fit for kings, soldiers, shepherds and stitched between farm chores, her costumes sow glad tidings cross-country.

The Shepherd Needed
SNEAKERS

BY LORI NESS, NEWARK, ILLINOIS

JEFF broke the news over supper—mumbling through his macaroni and cheese.

"Don't talk with your mouth full, son," I reminded, at the same time removing baby Amy's hand from her applesauce. "What did you say?"

Jeff rolled his eyes and took another mouthful. "I told Mrs. Sims I'd bring the sheep."

"Sheet?" I queried. "For a costume? Are you going to be an *angel* in the Christmas play?"

My husband, Dave, harrumphed. Jeff's older brother, Lance, laughed out loud. Jeff groaned. "Aw, Mom—we're not doing a play. We're going to have a pajunk."

"A what?"

"A pajunk. You know—we're going to act out the manger scene. Mrs. Sims said we needed animals, and I said I'd bring the sheep."

Now I understood. "Oh, a *pageant*! That's wonderful, dear. You said what?"

Jeff sighed. "I said I...uh, *we* would bring the sheep."

Dave harrumphed again. And Amy knocked her dish of applesauce on the floor.

Next morning the local newspaper had an announcement about the Live Nativity. Jeff was listed as a shepherd and animal contributor. I bought an armload of that issue and mailed them to out-of-town family and friends.

Jeff, usually a bit shy, strutted around with his head high...and spent hours grooming the three ewes he and Dave had selected from our flock.

The pageant took place on a very frosty Christmas Eve night. Jeff, Dave and Lance (who reluctantly agreed to don a fake beard and a bathrobe to help out) left early with the ewes in the truck.

By the time Amy and I arrived, quite a crowd had gathered in the fenced-in area on the church lawn. We found a place near the front of the large canvas tent, and

though the flaps were still closed, I could hear bleats and brays—and giggles—coming from within.

Dave ducked out from behind the flap and joined me, mopping a brow that was sweaty in spite of the cold.

"How's it going?" I asked.

"They're just about ready to begin," he informed. "Mrs. Sims is trying to get everybody posed. But the sheep aren't cooperating."

Just then, the tent flaps were drawn back, and an appreciative murmur ran through the crowd.

The creche featured Mary in a blue robe, Joseph in a crooked beard, and a straw-filled wooden manger holding a plump baby doll. Three Wise Men in cardboard crowns knelt in homage, and three bathrobed shepherds stood close by. A charcoal-colored burro was tethered on one side of the manger, and our ewes—looking nervous—were huddled on the other.

The children held their rigid postures, with varying expressions of awe and wonder at the miracle they beheld. Two little angels with wire and gauze wings came flitting around from behind the manger, and when the shepherds knelt in unison, spontaneous applause rippled through the onlookers.

Tears filled my eyes, blurring the edges of the scene. Amy clapped her chubby hands and waved at Jeff and Lance. Her brothers' eyes remained fixed on the manger.

As Pastor Matthews read the Christmas story, the photographer from the newspaper captured the scene on film. But when he focused in on the ewes, I noticed that one of them was hungrily eyeing an angel's wing and stretching its neck for a nibble. Uh, oh, I thought...

It was just as I feared! The surprised angel gave a yelp and dodged out of the way—knocking the other angel and one of the Wise Men off balance. The donkey brayed loudly and pulled away, tipping the manger...and the other ewes bolted for the parking lot. Jeff took off after one of them.

Lance sprang to his feet, tripped on his robe and fell on his face. He scrambled up again and, after a slippery sprint, made a diving tackle. A flurry of flakes followed. When the snow cleared, he was on his back, clutching the woolly ewe to his chest as the critter's legs pedaled frantically in the air. There was more applause.

Mrs. Sims, wringing her hands nervously, cued the choir to begin a chorus of *Away in a Manger*. After a moment, we onlookers joined in, and our voices quickly drowned out the commotion as the cast reassembled in the tent for the benediction.

The day after Christmas, there was a full page of color photos in the paper. I mailed out another batch—the picture of Lance holding the runaway ewe was right in the middle.

Sunday night over supper, Jeff had a bulletin. "Mrs. Sims says everyone liked the pajunk so much we're gonna do it again next year."

Dave winked at me and smiled to Jeff. "Maybe next time you boys had better wear your track shoes," he suggested.

Jeff forked up some mashed potatoes. "No problem, Dad," he assured around a mouthful. "Mrs. Sims made me promise that next year I'd bring a *camel*!"

SOURCE OF SEASON'S AT HAND

...In these homemade Nativities reverently displayed by families across the country this time of year.

Big or small, elaborate or simple, the heartfelt manger scenes— no matter what material they're made from—are a sincere reminder of the true reason we celebrate Christmas.

★ **TABLEAU MEANT TOGETHERNESS** *for Faye Oakes of Clinton, Ontario and her 13-year-old son, George—he cut out pine pieces and she painted them!*

★ **NOTHING FANCY** *went into this charming scene from Sharon Bonertz of Pincher Creek, Alberta...just "dough, brush hair curlers and imagination!" she smiles.*

★ **LIFE-SIZE SCENE** *shines in Nancy Packett's Appleton, Wisconsin yard—standing figures are 5 feet tall. Finishing them in time for season was big job, too. "I painted 16 hours a day!"*

★ **CARVED WITH CARE.** *"My father made this Nativity for my mother—it took him seven Christmases to complete," writes Cheryl Konkol, Appleton, Wisconsin.*

FRAGILE FAVORITE *was made by my husband, notes Nancy Richardson of Spring Grove, Illinois. His hobby is stained glass...he adds a piece per year.*

CROCHETED CRECHE *inspired Carol Mead of Los Alamos, New Mexico to learn craft—she made others for gifts, church.*

THREE KINGS *made of Styrofoam and terry cloth have honored spot in Marcie Williams' Croton, Ohio home. "I missed them when I lent them to church," she reports.*

WISE MEN—*macrame on wood dowels— have stood under tree for eight Christmases in Bonnie Pazdalski's Highland, Indiana home.*

NOVEL NATIVITY *has been part of several Christmases for Diane Simmler, Fryeburg, Maine, and her husband—Diane's aunt gave it to the couple the second year they were married.*

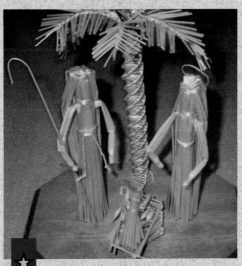

STRAW'S IN STALL—*and in the figures —that Lyla Schmitt of Gorham, Kansas weaves. They're made from wheat straw!*

THE BEST CHRISTMAS OF ALL

I do recall one Christmas Eve
More clearly than any other.
I was near the parlor
Just a-waiting for my mother
To open the off-limits room
So we could finally see
In all its lighted splendor
The blessed Christmas tree.

When Mother pulled away the sheet
My heart, I think, just stopped.
My brothers and my sisters
Stood with jaws completely dropped.
We saw that tinsel tower
Nearly bursting through the ceiling.
Its sparkling candle power
Made my eyes tear up with feeling.

Just then we heard a knocking
And my mother said, "Who is it?"
We heard a hearty "Ho, ho, ho"
And knew who'd come to visit.
In walked dear old Santa Claus—
His beard was long and white.
His coat was red, his boots were black
He was quite a sight!

He asked us kids if we'd been good
We promised that we had.
He handed out some toys and clothes
(No coal for being bad).
Then from his burlap bag he pulled
A small Nativity.
He placed the creche beneath the tree
for everyone to see.

Way up high, he placed a star
so bright it seemed to shine.
Then backing up, he smiled and said,
"Now that looks quite divine."
Then Santa held my hand in his
We all joined 'round the tree
And sang our favorite Christmas hymns
Not one, not two, but three!

Santa kissed my mother's cheek
and bid us all good night.
He said, "Be good 'til I return"
And then was out of sight.
Soon Dad walked in from working late
We told him what he'd missed—
Like Santa, singing and the star,
How Mother had been kissed!

"Yes, I saw Santa taking off,"
Our dad said with a grin.
"And if I'm not mistaken
He had a bearded chin."
We jumped with glee as Daddy laughed
And hugged us big and bearish.
That Christmas was the best of all,
A memory that I cherish!

By Lynda Penn, Bay View, Wisconsin

A 'Touching' Story...
ANGEL UNAWARE

BY JUANENE RHODES, OMRO, WISCONSIN

I've never forgotten a reenactment of the Nativity I once attended at our local church. The play was beautifully staged, realistic in every detail.

During the last moments on stage, a small angel in the front row, her halo amiss atop a tumble of red, curly hair, peered around a Wise Man at the baby in the manger. While those around her reverently sang *Silent Night*, the angel, blue eyes sparkling, timidly reached out to touch baby Jesus.

Raising a dubious eyebrow, the Wise Man cast warning glances at the wayward angel. Undeterred, she righted her crooked halo with one hand and continued reaching with the other.

Mary, kneeling at the manger's edge, moved aside as the awestruck angel continued her quest. The baby Jesus, having watched the angel's progression, giggled at the nearness of her. Squirming in obvious happiness, he reached out and grasped the angel's outstretched finger.

The incredulous look of joy on that tiny angel's face perfectly expressed the feelings of the whole congregation. For one fleeting moment, heaven and earth had touched...and neither would ever be the same again.

Lights Make Being Lost
JUST PURE BLISS!

BY DAVID FRAZIER

olks trying to find the tiny town of Bliss, Idaho during dark winter nights often end up at Dick and Karen Elliott's potato farm instead. That's because the Elliotts have so many Christmas lights some travelers think their place *is* Bliss!

Just how many lights are there? "Well…" Dick admits, "it's hard to keep track. I'd say there's somewhere between 12,000 and 14,000 bulbs.

"When it comes to Christmas lights, we just don't know when to stop," he adds with a grin. "Our son Mike and I start putting them up the day after Thanksgiving and just keep going!"

That has locals going out of their way most evenings to admire lights on the house, trees, bushes, fences and outbuildings…plus an illuminated Nativity scene, Ebenezer Scrooge and Santa Claus…elves climbing on

the TV satellite dish…and even a Wild West scene!

Lighting up the holidays for their neighbors warms the Elliotts' hearts. But it didn't always brighten their nights. "It got to the point where the lights inside the farmhouse dimmed whenever we had the Christmas lights on," Dick recalls.

"We had to have Idaho Power come out and put in a bigger transformer, plus separate electrical service for the display. It uses more 'juice' than the rest of the farm!"

Drawing that much power draws over 30 carloads of admirers each evening, and hundreds of those folks leave their cars and brave the cold for a closer look.

If you're looking for Bliss this holiday season—out on I-84 about 90 miles southeast of Boise—you might look for the Elliotts' place, too. Although their farm's well out of town, you'll be in bliss once you find it!

INDEX

O Tannenbaum! Betty (Hardt) Piepenbrink ponders pretty tree in the early 1940's. Wooden village and manger scene now grace her family's tree each Christmas.

YOU'RE INVITED! If you have an *original* recipe, story or craft you'd like us to consider for use in a future Christmas book, please send it (a good-quality photo of the craft project is fine) to "Christmas Book", Attn. Linda Piepenbrink, 5925 Country Lane, Greendale WI 53129. (Enclose a self-addressed stamped envelope if you want your material returned.)

Additional Photography By:
Joel Day, pp. 76-77
Ewing Galloway, p. 44
Robert Cushman Hayes, pp. 3, 4, 5, 78
Mike Huibregtse, pp. 42-43
Lynne B. Humkey, pp. 64-65
Jack Long, pp. 59, 72 and 81(bottom)
Larry G. McKee, p. 95
Gabe Palmer/Stock Market, p.9
Doyle Yoder, p. 47